POEMS OF
JUSTICE

▲▲▲▲▲▲▲▲▲▲▲▲

POEMS OF
JUSTICE

▲▲▲▲▲▲▲▲▲▲▲▲▲▲▲▲▲▲▲▲▲▲▲▲

Compiled by
THOMAS CURTIS CLARK

WILLETT, CLARK & COLBY
CHICAGO : 440 SOUTH DEARBORN STREET
NEW YORK : 200 FIFTH AVENUE
1929

To the Memory of
WALTER RAUSCHENBUSCH
Saint ― Seer
Social Prophet

ACKNOWLEDGMENTS

▲▲▲▲▲▲▲▲▲▲▲▲

Acknowledgment is here made of the generous co-operation of both contributing poets and publishers in the bringing together of this anthology. The compiler has made every effort to trace the ownership of copyrighted poems, and necessary permissions have been secured. Should there prove to be any question regarding the use of any poem, regret is here expressed for such error. Upon notification of any such oversight, proper acknowledgment will be made in future editions.

Detailed acknowledgment to publishers and poets will be found in the closing pages of the book.

Special gratitude is here expressed to the following persons, who have cooperated in making this anthology, in the suggestion of poems to be included, special favors in connection with included poems, assistance in the preparing of the manuscript, etc.: Zona Gale, Upton Sinclair, Edwin Markham, Mrs. Walter Rauschenbusch, Harriet Monroe, Carl Sandburg, John Haynes Holmes, Harry F. Ward, Vida D. Scudder, William J. Colby, Caroline M. Hill, Fred Merrifield, Sarah Cleghorn, Henry van Dyke, Graham Taylor, Francis J. McConnell, Lucia Trent, Charles Erskine Scott Wood, Alva W. Taylor, Ralph Cheyney, Robert Whitaker, Ruth Hunt, Clement Wood, Charlotte Perkins Gilman, Hazel Davis Clark,

ACKNOWLEDGMENTS

▲

Henry Harrison, Sidney Strong, Vachel Lindsay, W. H. Murray, Robert Haven Schauffler, Florence Wilkinson Evans, Charles Hanson Towne, Arthur E. White, Jr., Hermann Hagedorn, James Oppenheim, John Curtis Underwood, Solon De Leon, and Robert E. Clark.

THE COMPILER

CONTENTS

PART ONE

PANORAMA OF THE POOR

1
▼

PART TWO

THE MARCH OF REVOLT

45
▼

PART THREE

BROTHERS ALL

135
▼

PART FOUR

DREAMS AND GOALS

193
▼

INDEXES

281
▼

FOREWORD

BY

ZONA GALE

Every poet, every artist sees more man, more woman, more tree, more water, more world than do others. They are poets and artists because they do have this heightened perception of life and love, of objects and human relationships, of crises and of the commonplace. To be a poet means to be one who is sensitized to every aspect of the human scene, and who in music can tell of his insight.

Then naturally poets have a highly developed sensitiveness toward human suffering. They have a seer's sense of the stupidity and cruelty of man's dealing with man. More than this, they have a profound emotional sense not merely of indignation and compassion, but of fellowship with the trampled and wasted ones. Finally, their genius being creative, poets apply creative genius to a dream of a world where human beings act their human parts, instead of impersonating ape and tiger, lion, or even lamb. It is their exquisite province to do this beautifully, and in music.

All the poets of importance of all time have written poetry of social justice. To write of field, flower, feathered thing, mosaic and fabric, ivory, ape and peacock is their heritage; but it is also their power to write of "man as god" in a pit, as a being doomed by his fellows to the use of a fraction of his intelligence, stunted, limited, cribbed, dying of the malady of life when he had groped for his gateway.

This collection of Poems of Justice contains the word of innumerable voices from old days to the present. From Isaiah to Greenwich Village is a long lane, but that lane stretches, filled with the singers of one theme. The handling is didactic or lyric, reasoned or passionate; but all is charged with an energy like the energy of atoms.

Whatever is to run through the ages continuing to change human nature, and claiming to adjust relationships according to economic formulæ, it is sure that these singers have leaped beyond law and formulæ, and they *know*. Of social justice, like other magics, "poets have always known." The world of which they tell is a world of reality, waiting to be realized. "*Undoubtedly man will outgrow his sufferings*," a wise man * said, and he said also: "*Everything is a thought first*."

* C. F. Gale

POEMS OF
JUSTICE

▲▲▲▲▲▲▲▲▲▲▲▲▲

PANORAMA OF
THE POOR

▼

In the Market-Place

In Babylon, high Babylon,
  What gear is bought and sold?
All merchandise beneath the sun
  That bartered is for gold;
Amber and oils from far beyond
  The desert and the fen,
And wines whereof our throats are fond —
  Yea! and the souls of men!

In Babylon, gray Babylon,
  What goods are sold and bought?
Vesture of linen subtly spun,
  And cups from agate wrought;
Raiment of many-colored silk
  For some fair denizen,
And ivory more white than milk —
  Yea! and the souls of men! . . .

In Babylon, sad Babylon,
  What chattels shall invite?
A wife whenas your youth is done,
  Or leman for a night.
Before Astarte's portico
  The torches flare again;
The shadows come, the shadows go —
  Yea! and the souls of men!

George Sterling

From " Beyond the Breakers "

[1]

Manhattan

Here in the furnace City, in the humid air they faint,
  God's pallid poor, His people, with scarcely space for
      breath;
So foul their teeming houses, so full of shame and taint,
  They cannot crowd within them for the frightful
      fear of Death.

Yet somewhere, Lord, Thine open seas are singing with
      the rain,
  And somewhere underneath Thy stars the cool waves
      crash and beat;
Why is it here, and only here, are huddled Death and
      Pain,
  And here the form of Horror stalks, a menace in the
      street!

The burning flagstones gleam like glass at morning and
      at noon,
  The giant walls shut out the breeze — if any breeze
      should blow;
And high above the smothering town at midnight hangs
      the moon,
  A red medallion in the sky, a monster cameo.

Charles Hanson Towne

A Cry from the Ghetto

The roaring of the wheels has filled my ears,
  The clashing and the clamor shut me in;
Myself, my soul, in chaos disappears,
  I cannot think or feel amid the din.
Toiling and toiling and toiling — endless toil.

JUSTICE

For whom? For what? Why should the work be
    done?
I do not ask, or know. I only toil.
    I work until the day and night are one.

The clock above me ticks away the day,
    Its hands are spinning, spinning, like the wheels.
It cannot sleep or for a moment stay,
    It is a thing like me, and does not feel.
It throbs as though my heart were beating there —
    A heart? My heart? I know not what it means.
The clock ticks, and below I strive and stare.
    And so we lose the hour. We are machines.

Noon calls a truce, an ending to the sound,
    As if a battle had one moment stayed —
A bloody field! The dead lie all around;
    Their wounds cry out until I grow afraid.
It comes — the signal! See, the dead men rise,
    They fight again, amid the roar they fight.
Blindly, and knowing not for whom, or why,
    They fight, they fall, they sink into the night.

Yet somewhere, God, drenched roses bloom by fountains
      draped with mist
    In old, lost gardens of the earth made lyrical with rain;
Why is it here a million brows by hungry Death are
      kissed,
    And here is packed, one Summer night, a whole
    world's fiery pain!

Morris Rosenfeld

Translated from the Yiddish by C. W. Linn

[3]

BROADWAY

How like the stars are these white, nameless faces —
   These far innumerable burning coals!
This pale procession out of stellar spaces,
   This Milky Way of souls!
Each in its own bright nebulæ enfurled,
Each face, dear God, a world!

I fling my gaze out through the silent night:
   In those far stars, what gardens, what high halls
Has mortal yearning built for its delight,
   What chasms and what walls?
What quiet mansions where a soul may dwell?
What heaven and what hell?

Hermann Hagedorn

IN A SWEATSHOP

Pent in, and sickening for one wholesome draught
Of air — God's gift that cities sell so dear —
They stitch and stitch. The dim lights fall upon
Bent bodies, hollowed bosoms and dead eyes.
Their very mirth is horrible to hear,
It is so joyless! Every needle-stroke
Knits into dainty fabrics that shall go
Where Fashion flaunts, the protest and the pain
Of ravaged lives, of souls denied their food.
At last the clock-stroke! From the beetling shop
The prisoners file, and up and down the street
Scatter to hutches humorists call Home,
To sin, to die, or, if it may be, clutch
Some pleasure fierce enough to drown the thought
That on the morrow they must meet again.

Richard Burton

[4]

Paper Roses

"How camest thou by thy roses, Child?"
　"I toiled at them in a little room."
"Thy window flaming with the dawn?"
　"Nay, master; 'twas in fearful gloom."

"What gave thy rose its color, then?"
　"My cheek's blood, as I bent my head."
"Thy cheek is cold and lifeless, Child."
　"Mayhap it was my heart that bled."

"One white rose in thy basket, Child?"
　"Aye, master, that's to crown the whole."
"What is it, then, O Little Child?"
　"Mayhap . . . mayhap it is my soul!"

Dana Burnet

Mill Children

We have forgotten how to sing: our laughter is a godless
　thing: listless and loud and shrill and sly.
We have forgotten how to smile. Our lips, our voices
　too are vile. We are all dead before we die.

Our mothers' mothers made us so: the father that we
　never know in blindness and in wantonness
Caused us to come to question you. What is it that you
　others do, that profit so by our distress?

You and your children softly sleep. We and our mothers
　vigil keep. You cheated us of all delight,
Ere our sick spirits came to birth: you made our fair and
　fruitful earth a nest of pestilence and blight.

Your black machines are never still, and hard, relentless
    as your will, they card us like the cotton waste.
And flesh and blood more cheap than they, they seize and
    eat and shred away, to feed the fever of your haste.

For we are waste and shoddy here, who know no God,
    no faith but fear, no happiness, no hope but sleep.
Half imbecile and half obscene we sit and tend each tense
    machine, too sick to sigh, too tired to weep,
Until the tortured end of day, when fevered faces turn
    away, to see the stars from blackness leap.

John Curtis Underwood

THE LITTLE CHILDREN

Sadly through the factory doors
    The little children pass,
They do not like to leave behind
    The morning sky and grass.

All day the wheels will eat their joy
    And turn it into gold,
And when they pass the doors again
    The world will seem so old!

Irwin Granich

FACTORIES

Buried in one-eyed dungeons where the walls
Stare out on other walls through window-panes,
A grinding mechanism squats and chains
Each arm and leg to slavish rituals,
The while monotonous privation hauls
Dark bodies to and fro down prison lanes

▲

Where no soft light nor open door remains
To proffer freedom from such funerals.

The eye peering from out each socket there
Reflects a roving madman in a cave
Striving and straining to burst the stony shell:
The look makes every cell begin to glare,
The very walls to shudder and to rave,
As each grim puppet earns his bread in hell.

Alfred Kreymborg

SONG OF A FACTORY GIRL

It's hard to breathe in a tenement hall,
   So I ran to the little park,
As a lover runs from a crowded ball
   To the moonlit dark.

I drank in clear air as one will
   Who is doomed to die,
Wistfully watching from a hill
   The unmarred sky.

And the great trees bowed in their gold and red
   Till my heart caught flame;
And my soul, that I thought was crushed or dead,
   Uttered a name.

I hadn't called the name of God —
   For a long time;
But it stirred in me as the seed in sod,
   Or a broken rhyme.

Marya Zaturensky

[7]

From Our Lady of Idleness

They in the darkness gather and ask
Her name, the mistress of their endless task.

   The Toilers:
Tinsel-makers in factory gloom,
Miners in ethylene pits,
Divers and druggists mixing poisonous bloom;

Huge hunters, men of brawn,
Half-naked creatures of the tropics,
Furred trappers stealing forth at Labrador dawn;

Catchers of beetles, sheep-men in bleak sheds,
Pearl-fishers perched on Indian coasts,
Children in stifling towers pulling threads;

Dark bunchy women pricking intricate laces,
Myopic jewelers' apprentices,
Arabs who chase the long-legged birds in sandy
      places:

They are her invisible slaves,
The genii of her costly wishes,
Climbing, descending, running under waves.

They strip earth's dimmest cell,
They burn and drown and stifle
To build her inconceivable and fragile shell.

Florence Wilkinson Evans

▲

THE INCENTIVE

I saw a sickly cellar plant
Droop on its feeble stem, for want
Of sun and wind and rain and dew —
Of freedom! — Then a man came through
The cellar, and I heard him say,
" Poor, foolish plant, by all means stay
Contented here; for — know you not? —
This stagnant dampness, mold and rot
Are your incentive to grow tall
And reach that sunbeam on the wall."
— Even as he spoke, the sun's one spark
Withdrew, and left the dusk more dark.

Sarah N. Cleghorn

THE FUGITIVES

We are they that go, that go,
Plunging before the hidden blow.
We run the byways of the earth,
For we are fugitive from birth,
Blindfolded, with wide hands abroad
That sow, that sow the sullen sod.

We cannot wait, we cannot stop
For flushing field or quickened crop;
The orange bow of dusky dawn
Glimmers our smoking swath upon;
Blindfolded still we hurry on.

How do we know the ways we run
That are blindfolded from the sun?
We stagger swiftly to the call,
Our wide hands feeling for the wall.

[9]

Oh, ye who climb to some clear heaven,
By grace of day and leisure given,
Pity us, fugitive and driven —
The lithe whip curling on our track,
The headlong haste that looks not back!

Florence Wilkinson Evans

SEEDLINGS

My mother was a sweat-shop slave, her breast
  Was black with sores. She had no thought of me
  When she conceived, and so I came to be,
In ignorance, the bastard of incest.
  I live in slums where dirt and crime are rife.
Some day the rotten tissues of my brain
Will burst, and I will wander forth insane
  And blindly I will wreak revenge on life.
The perfumed ladies of the sheltered class
Will pray, and dutifully go to mass;
  But they will never stoop to cleanse the earth
  Of that foul thing which putrified my birth.
Have they not blossomed from the wage-slave's need —
White flowers of the soil wherein I breed?

Mary Craig Sinclair

TONIGHT

Tonight the beautiful, chaste moon
  From heaven's height
Scatters over the bridal earth
  Blossoms of white;
And spring's renewed glad charms unfold
  Endless delight.

Such mystic wonder the hushed world wears,
    Evil has fled
Far, far away; in every heart
    God reigns instead. . . .
Tonight a starving virgin sells
    Her soul for bread.

Carlos Wupperman

LIFE IS A FEAST, THEY SAY

Life is a feast, they say:
Yet millions of people are born hungry and die
    hungry —
And, dying, wonder why they ever had to live.

Life is a feast, they say:
Yet millions of women pass their years
Without seeing a country road or a field of clover.

Life is a feast, they say:
Yet millions of children, having glutted their eyes before
    a bright-colored Christmas window,
Go home, heart-hungry, to a dark corner of a black
    wall, by Tenement Alley.

Life is a feast, they say.

Thomas Curtis Clark

THE SHADOW-CHILD

Why do the wheels go whirring round,
    Mother, mother?
O mother, are they giants bound,
    And will they growl forever?

[11]

Yes, fiery giants underground,
  Daughter, little daughter,
Forever turn the wheels around,
  And rumble-grumble ever.

Why do I pick the threads all day,
  Mother, mother?
While sunshine children are at play?
  And must I work forever?

Yes, shadow-child; the livelong day,
  Daughter, little daughter,
Your hands must pick the threads away,
  And feel the sunshine never.

Why do the birds sing in the sun,
  Mother, mother,
If all day long I run and run,
  Run with the wheels forever?

The birds may sing till day is done,
  Daughter, little daughter,
But with the wheels your feet must run —
  Run with the wheels forever.

Why do I feel so tired each night,
  Mother, mother?
The wheels are always buzzing bright;
  Do they grow sleepy never?

O baby-thing, so soft and white,
  Daughter, little daughter,
The big wheels grind us in their might,
  And they will grind forever.

And is the white thread never spun,
  Mother, mother?

And is the white cloth never done,
　For you and me done never?

Oh, yes, our thread will all be spun,
　Daughter, little daughter,
When we lie down out in the sun,
　And work no more forever.

And when will come that happy day,
　Mother, mother?
Oh, shall we laugh and sing and play,
　Out in the sun forever?

No, shadow-child, we'll rest all day,
　Daughter, little daughter,
Where green grass grows and roses gay,
　There in the sun forever.

Harriet Monroe

THE WOLF AT THE DOOR

There's a haunting horror near us
　That nothing drives away;
Fierce lamping eyes at nightfall,
　A crouching shade by day;
There's a whining at the threshold,
　There's a scratching at the floor.
To work! To work! In Heaven's name!
　The wolf is at the door!

The day was long, the night was short,
　The bed was hard and cold;
Still weary are the little ones,
　Still weary are the old.

JUSTICE

We are weary in our cradles
  From our mother's toil untold;
We are born to hoarded weariness
  As some to hoarded gold.

We will not rise! We will not work!
  Nothing the day can give
Is half so sweet as an hour of sleep;
  Better to sleep than live!
What power can stir these heavy limbs?
  What hope these dull hearts swell?
What fear more cold, what pain more sharp
  Than the life we know so well? . . .

The slow, relentless, padding step
  That never goes astray —
The rustle in the underbrush —
  The shadow in the way —
The straining flight — the long pursuit —
  The steady gain behind —
Death-wearied man and tireless brute,
  And the struggle wild and blind!

There's a hot breath at the keyhole
  And a tearing as of teeth!
Well do I know the bloodshot eyes
  And the dripping jaws beneath!
There's a whining at the threshold —
  There's a scratching at the floor —
To work! To work! In Heaven's name!
  The wolf is at the door!

                          Charlotte Perkins Gilman

PITTSBURGH

Over his face his gray hair drifting hides his Labor-glory
    in smoke,
Strange through his breath the soot is sifting, his feet are
    buried in coal and coke.
By night hands twisted and lurid in fires, by day hands
    blackened with grime and oil,
He toils at the foundries and never tires, and ever and
    ever his lot is toil.

He speeds his soul till his body wrestles with terrible
    tonnage and terrible time,
Out through the yards and over the trestles the flat-cars
    clank and the engines chime,
His mills through windows seem eaten with fire, his high
    cranes travel, his ingots roll,
And billet and wheel and whistle and wire shriek with
    the speeding up of his soul.

Lanterns with reds and greens a-glisten wave the way
    and the head-light glares,
The back-bent laborers glance and listen and out through
    the night the tail-light flares —
Deep in the mills like a tipping cradle the huge converter
    turns on its wheel
And sizzling spills in the ten-ton ladle a golden water of
    molten steel.

Yet screwed with toil his low face searches shadow-
    edged fires and whited pits,
Gripping his levers his body lurches, grappling his irons
    he prods and hits,
And deaf with the roll and clangor and rattle with its
    sharp escaping staccato of steam,

And blind with flame and worn with battle, into his
    tonnage he turns his dream.

The world he has builded rises around us, our wonder-
    cities and weaving rails,
Over his wires a marvel has found us, a glory rides in our
    wheeléd mails,
For the Earth grows small with strong Steel woven, and
    they come together who plotted apart —
But he who has wrought this thing in his oven knows
    only toil and the tired heart.

James Oppenheim

From SMOKE AND STEEL

  A bar of steel — it is only
Smoke at the heart of it, smoke and the blood of a man.
A runner of fire ran in it, ran out, ran somewhere else,
And left — smoke and the blood of a man
And the finished steel, chilled and blue.
So fire runs in, runs out, runs somewhere else again,
And the bar of steel is a gun, a wheel, a nail, a shovel,
A rudder under the sea, a steering-gear in the sky;
And always dark in the heart and through it,
Smoke and the blood of a man.
Pittsburgh, Youngstown, Gary — they make their steel
    with men.

Carl Sandburg

L'HOMME MACHINE

Stoking, stoking, stoking —
Days of dusty night;
Stoking, stoking, stoking —
Lit with red hell's light.

[16]

Pouring, pouring, pouring —
  Ladling wealth untold;
Pouring, pouring, pouring —
  Metal gods to mold.

Molding, molding, molding —
  Lives of men inwrought;
Molding, molding, molding —
  Men with steel are bought.

Helen Seaman

HYMN OF HALSTED STREET

When the young moon faints over Halsted Street
  In a sultry, sullen sky,
I hear the beat of alien feet
  And watch the world go by.

I hear the beat of alien feet
  And the lilt of an alien song,
Through the lifeless air of the littered street
  Clangs loud a brazen gong! . . .

They have banished Beauty from Halsted Street,
  They have banished the clean, green ways;
The children shout in the noisome heat
  Or fret through the strident days.

And youth philanders in Halsted Street —
  But never a tree nor shrine,
Nor a stone to the dead, nor a fountain sweet,
  Nor hint of blossoming vine

Endears the crossways — nor any prayers
  For peace, nor old bells' chime;

[17]

JUSTICE

Men gamble in brazen or bitter wares —
    For the rest, no time, no time!

" Big Bargains " flourish in Halsted Street,
    Hardware and other things,
But the sky is a dead moon's winding-sheet
    And the air is too thick for wings!

The ice-cream man from Calabria
    Rubs shoulders with Gypsy and Jew,
And matzos with dates from Arabia —
    And the ancient dissolves in the new. . . .

While the dreams of Age turn to Thessaly
    Or Attic fields of corn,
Or to sunny vineyards of Sicily,
    The honk of a motor horn

Stirs the thoughts of Youth to some victory
    In the trampled glooms of France,
From dismal toil in a factory
    To that girl at last night's dance! . . .

There are widows who weep in Halsted Street,
    There are Jews who barter and save,
But the New World clangs with a heartless beat,
    And the Old has found a grave! . . .

When the sick moon dies over Halsted Street
    In her smoky bed of sky,
The funeral feet of the people beat
    An alien, ancient cry!

Brent Dow Allinson

THE RUSSIAN IMMIGRANT GRANDMOTHER

As wrinkled as the wind-swept firth,
  And weather-browned the brow;
Broad hands that grubbed the sprouting earth
  In young years, hazy now.

Mother of rugged-muscled men
  Who wield the iron tool,
And free-limbed women who again
  Fulfill the iron rule.

To bear unto the master-male
  Full procreation's store,
Plodding within the subject pale
  Unto the mystic door.

Old mother, Russian-kerchiefed, blent
  Of power and meek defeat,
I hear thy woman's dumb lament
  Upon our city street.

Fanny Bixby Spencer

I AM THE IMMIGRANT

Since the dawn of creation my restless feet have beaten
  new paths across the earth.
My uneasy bark has tossed on all seas.
My wanderlust was born of the craving for more liberty
  and a better wage for the sweat of my face.
I looked toward the United States with eyes kindled by
  the fire of ambition and heart quickened with new-
  born hope.
I approached its gates with great expectation.
I entered in it with fine hope.

[19]

▲

I have shouldered my burden as the American man-of all-work.
I contribute eighty-five per cent of all the labor in the slaughtering and meat-packing industries.
I do seven-tenths of the bituminous coal mining.
I do seventy-eight per cent of all the work in the woolen mills.
I contribute nine-tenths of all the labor in the cotton mills.
I make nineteen-twentieths of all the clothing.
I manufacture more than half the shoes.
I build four-fifths of all the furniture.
I make half of the collars, cuffs and shirts.
I turn out four-fifths of all the leather.
I make half the gloves.
I refine nearly nineteen-twentieths of the sugar.
And yet, I am the great American problem.

Author Unknown

CHRIST ON MADISON STREET

I looked for Christ on Madison Street
Where men went by with stumbling feet,
Where heads were bowed in the darkness there
Of gray clouds hanging low in the air.
I looked for Him, a vision of white —
But gay burlesques with their crimson light
Have led my steps to a darker place
Where smoke of passion hid Christ's face.
I looked for Christ in the hidden skies,
A flaming vision to blind my eyes —
While Christ walked by with stumbling feet
Along with the men of Madison Street.

Raymond Kresensky

STREET WINDOW

The pawn-shop man knows hunger,
And how far hunger has eaten the heart
Of one who comes with an old keepsake.
Here are wedding rings and baby bracelets,
Scarf pins, and shoe buckles, jeweled garters,
Old-fashioned knives with inlaid handles,
Watches of old gold and silver,
Old coins worn with finger-marks.
They tell stories.

Carl Sandburg

WE MAKE IRON IN BIRMINGHAM

We make iron in Birmingham.
Damn the rest:
We make iron.

We fling up noises that shriek in the sky;
We glut the clouds with smoke,
And the sun filters faintly through.

Our cats, and sparrows, and buildings are smutty.
Our trees stand naked and black,
Like bony Negro women.

We don't seem to mind the quiet moon
That eases across the tops of the buildings;
Nor the sun that sets soft down the L&N tracks.
We don't seem to mind.

We make iron in Birmingham.
Damn the rest.

Karl C. Harrison

JUSTICE

From Out of the Coalfields

Beauty never visits mining places,
For the yellow smoke taints the summer air.
Despair graves lines on the dwellers' faces,
My fellows' faces, for my fellows live there.

There by the wayside dusty weed drowses,
The darnel and dock and starwort run rife;
Gaunt folk stare from the doors of the houses,
Folk with no share in the beauty of life.

There on slag-heaps, where no bird poises,
My fellows' wan children tumble and climb,
Playing in the dust, making shrill noises,
Sweet human flowers that will fade ere their time.

Playing in the slag with thin white faces,
Where headstocks loom by the railway lines —
Round-eyed children cheated of life's graces —
My fellows' children, born for the mines.

Frederick C. Boden

China Town, San Francisco

Here are the faces of women;
Young women,
Old women.
They peer at me
From the dark by the way
And clutch at my sleeve
As I pass.

Here are the women that men forget;
Young women,
Old women.

D. Maitland Bushby

The Lean Gray Rats

The lean gray rats of hunger
    Have gnawed my soul in twain;
Till cursing the God that made it,
    The good half died in pain.

The ill half lived and prospered,
    Waxed brutal and strong and fat;
But the good half died and was eaten
    In hell by a lean gray rat.

Skipwith Cannell

Faces

Each morning, faces, faces, faces;
Each day new faces — old faces new with meaning;
Each day, what a world of faces!

    .   .   .   .   .

Faces of mothers and babies on hot days, with a hundred
    needs eliciting pity but baffling the soul for help
    and sympathy;
Wistful faces of street urchins hungrily scanning the
    face of the rich man's pampered chick, wallowing
    in El Dorado opulence;
Faces of country people looking out of trains at the
    railway depots — with eyes like quiet cattle and
    chewing, chewing, as cattle chew cud, faces simple,
    freckled, unconsciously humorous, drooping before
    the gaze of strangers, some care-lined, sin-marked
    and latent with burden-weariness, inscrutable,
    human faces the essence of our democracy;
Faces of unborn babies that cheated mother's kiss and
    caress;

What a world of faces!
Faces which pity themselves; ostrich-like faces buried
    in a mask of sand; junk-pile faces gathering every-
    thing that comes along; shifty faces refusing your
    face. . . .
What a world of faces!

Cyprus R. Mitchell

INVOCATION

    Lord, give us strength!
Beneath this tumbled mass of reeking walls —
Brute brick and lime, our buried spirit calls —
    Lord, give us strength!

    Lean down and save!
Through sunless catacombs of hopeless hope,
Dead dreams, and utter weariness we grope —
    Lean down and save!

    Help us to rise!
We clamor at the bars of freedom, run
Through starless darkness; Oh, the Sun, the Sun!
    Help us to rise!

David George Plotkin

DAWN AFTER CHRISTMAS

Hag-haunted men who stare too long at rivers,
    Stoop-shouldered girls who weep too much o' nights,
What line marks off the takers from the givers
    In our confusing world of wrongs and rights?

The lamp posts, dribbling light on foggy byways,
    Know tales too dark for sons of men to tell;
And cobblestones along forgotten highways
    Have clanged to Death, the deathless sentinel.

This Christmas cheer within is reassuring;
    Our women have warm hands and tender eyes;
But there outside the shadows wait, enduring,
    And ghosts in ambush mock our paradise.
Tonight the Prince of Peace has banished sorrow;
Tomorrow lurks around the turn . . . Tomorrow!

Elias Lieberman

PLOWMEN

God made a race of plowmen
    And gave them earth to till,
To mold and make and plow, then
    To harvest with a will.

He set a star to guide them,
    A green tree for its shade,
The cawing crows to chide them
    And steal what they had made.

He sent the sun to burn them,
    The cooling touch of rain;
Each waking dawn to turn them
    Back to their plows again.

He gave them seed for sowing,
    A day in which to sow,
Then sent them forth to mowing
    With mighty wills to mow.

God made a race of plowmen
   And gave them earth to till,
To sow and reap and plow, then
   Leave them plowmen still.

Howard McKinley Corning

WOMAN PLOWING

She, being married to the Soil
   So long, has never known
A lover who would give her bread
   To eat, instead of stone.

Day after day she wonders, as
   She plows with low-bowed head,
Why furrows make an endless grave
   For all her dreams, born dead.

Oh, she would gladly lie with Death
   And yield him blood and bone —
But he'd return her to the Soil,
   Forever as his own.

Robert Liddell Lowe

PRISON

The prison stands upon a hill,
Ominously bleak and still;

And every stone we know to be
Mortared with hypocrisy;

Chiseled in the bitter name
Of our cruelty and shame.

[26]

▲

We, who herd these prisoners
Like a pack of beaten curs,

We have made the world where they
Have been lost or gone astray.

Our failures glare like hideous scars
From these ugly prison bars.

Ours is the sin of those who wait
By the never-turning gate,

And ours the crime of those who sway
Lifeless in the faltering day.

Lucia Trent

THE NEGRO

I am the Negro:
Black as the night is black,
Black like the depths of my Africa.

I've been a slave:
Caesar told me to keep his door-steps clean.
I brushed the boots of Washington.

I've been a worker:
Under my hand the pyramids arose.
I made mortar for the Woolworth Building.

I've been a singer:
All the way from Africa to Georgia I carried my sorrow
songs.
I made ragtime.

I've been a victim:
The Belgians cut off my hands in the Congo.
They lynch me now in Texas.

[27]

I am a Negro:
Black as the night is black,
Black like the depths of my Africa.

Langston Hughes

BLACK MAGDALENS

These have no Christ to spit and stoop
  To write upon the sand,
Inviting him that has not sinned
  To raise the first rude hand.

And if He came they could not buy
  Rich ointment for His feet;
The body's sale scarce yields enough
  To let the body eat.

The chaste clean ladies pass them by
  And draw their skirts aside,
But Magdalens have a ready laugh;
  They wrap their wounds in pride.

They fare full ill since Christ forsook
  The cross to mount a throne,
And Virtue still is stooping down
  To cast the first hard stone.

Countee Cullen

LONDON

I wander through each chartered street,
  Near where the chartered Thames does flow;
A mark in every face I meet,
  Marks of weakness, marks of woe.

In every cry of every man,
　In every infant's cry of fear,
In every voice, in every ban,
　The mind-forged manacles I hear:

How the chimney-sweeper's cry
　Every blackening church appalls,
And the hapless soldier's sigh
　Runs in blood down palace-walls.

But most, through midnight streets I hear
　How the youthful harlot's curse
Blasts the new-born infant's tear,
　And blights with plagues the marriage-hearse.

William Blake

Fleet Street Eclogues

I, too, for light the world explore,
　And, trembling, tread where angels trod;
Devout at every shrine adore,
　And follow after each new god.

But by the altar everywhere
　I find the money-changer's stall;
And littering every temple-stair
　The sick and sore like maggots crawl. . . .

And always divers undertones
　Within the roaring tempest throb —
The chink of gold, the laborer's groans,
　The infant's wail, the woman's sob.

Hoarsely they beg of Fate to give
　A little lightening of their woe,
A little time to love, to live,
　A little time to think and know.

JUSTICE

I see where from the slums may rise
  Some unexpected dreadful dawn —
The gleam of steeled and scowling eyes,
  A flash of women's faces wan!

John Davidson

From THE POEMS OF WEST HAM

From a high place I saw the city
Open and bare below me spread,
And therein walked (O God of pity!)
Few living, many dead.

Dead men entombed in daily labors,
Grappling for gold in ghostly strife;
Dead neighbors chattering to dead neighbors;
And dead youth — seeing life.

Dead women decking lifeless bodies
(See, what a gay and lovely shroud!)
And in rich temples, where no God is,
Dead corpses, praying loud.

But, oh, my eyes were ever turning,
With joy and tender deep delight
To where, like stars in dark skies burning,
The living souls shone bright.

Where are her priestly hands preparing
Holy mother and happy wife?
Daily her humble home is sharing
The bread and wine of life.

The neighbors seek her fireside, telling
Of sacred sorrow, joyous plan;

[30]

And often quietly in her dwelling
Meet with the Son of Man.

See where the craftsman's last touch lingers
To draw the wonder from the wood,
As life and love, poured through his fingers,
Create and call it good.

. . . . .

Yonder a youth, afire with pity,
Cries in the press most passionately,
" Comrades, arise! and build a city
Fit dwelling for the free! "

He cries. The dead men pass. The pavement
Echoes his voice. Yet, if one stay,
Hope whispers that one opening grave meant
A resurrection day!

There a stern gray-haired prophet preaches
To proud pews full of dull and dead;
And there a gentle schoolma'am teaches
With glory round her head.

Many the dead, and few the living?
Yet see life springing everywhere —
Leaping from soul to soul, and giving
A pause to our despair.

And comes the wind of God's voice sweeping —
" Blind seer, behold again! for they,
Whom you called dead men, are but sleeping
And shall awake one day! "

Author Unknown

The Song of the Shirt

With fingers weary and worn,
　With eyelids heavy and red,
A woman sat in unwomanly rags,
　Plying her needle and thread —
Stitch! stitch! stitch!
　In poverty, hunger and dirt,
And still with a voice of dolorous pitch
　She sang the " Song of the Shirt! "

" Work! work! work!
　While the cock is crowing aloof!
And work — work — work,
　Till the stars shine through the roof!
It's oh! to be a slave
　Along with the barbarous Turk,
Where a woman has never a soul to save,
　If this is Christian work!

" Work — work — work
　Till the brain begins to swim;
Work — work — work
　Till the eyes are heavy and dim!
Seam, and gusset, and band,
　Band, and gusset, and seam,
Till over the buttons I fall asleep,
　And sew them on in a dream!

" O men, with sisters dear!
　O men, with mothers and wives!
It is not linen you're wearing out,
　But human creatures' lives!
Stitch — stitch — stitch!
　In poverty, hunger and dirt —

Sewing at once, with a double thread,
    A shroud as well as a shirt!

" But why do I talk of Death —
    That phantom of grisly bone?
I hardly fear his terrible shape,
    It seems so like my own —
    It seems so like my own
Because of the fasts I keep;
    O God! that bread should be so dear,
And flesh and blood so cheap!

.   .   .   .   .

" Oh, but to breathe the breath
    Of the cowslip and primrose sweet —
With the sky above my head,
    And the grass beneath my feet!
For only one short hour
    To feel as I used to feel,
Before I knew the woes of want
    And the walk that costs a meal!

" Oh, but for one short hour —
    A respite, however brief!
No blessed leisure for love or hope,
    But only time for grief!
A little weeping would ease my heart;
    But in their briny bed
My tears must stop, for every drop
    Hinders needle and thread! "

With fingers weary and worn,
    With eyelids heavy and red,
A woman sat in unwomanly rags,
    Plying her needle and thread —

Stitch! stitch! stitch!
In poverty, hunger and dirt;
And still with a voice of dolorous pitch —
Would that its tone could reach the rich! —
She sang the " Song of the Shirt."

Thomas Hood

THE CHILDREN'S AUCTION

Who bids for the little children —
Body, and soul and brain?
Who bids for the little children —
Young and without a stain?
" Will no one bid," said England,
" For their souls so pure and white,
And fit for all good or evil
The world on their page may write? "

" We bid," said Pest and Famine;
" We bid for life and limb;
Fever and pain and squalor,
Their bright young eyes shall dim.
When the children grow too many,
We'll nurse them as our own,
And hide them in secret places
Where none may hear their moan."

" I bid," said Beggary, howling;
" I bid for them one and all!
I'll teach them a thousand lessons —
To lie, to skulk, to crawl!
They shall sleep in my lair like maggots,
They shall rot in the fair sunshine;
And if they serve my purpose
I hope they'll answer thine."

[34]

▲

" I'll bid you higher and higher,"
  Said Crime, with a wolfish grin;
" For I love to lead the children
  Through the pleasant paths of sin.
They shall swarm in the streets to pilfer
  They shall plague the broad highway,
They shall grow too old for pity
  And ripe for the law to slay.

" Give me the little children,
  Ye good, ye rich, ye wise,
And let the busy world spin round
  While ye shut your idle eyes;
And your judges shall have work,
  And your lawyers wag the tongue,
And the jailers and policemen
  Shall be fathers to the young! "

Charles Mackay

PIPER, PLAY!

Now the furnaces are out,
  And the aching anvils sleep:
Down the road the grimy rout
  Tramples homeward twenty deep.
    Piper, play! Piper, play!
      For a little we are free!
      Foot it girls and shake your curls,
        Haggard creatures though we be!

Bridled looms delay their din;
  All the humming wheels are spent;
Busy spindles cease to spin;
  Warp and woof must rest content.

[35]

Piper, play! Piper, play!
For a little we are free!
Foot it girls and shake your curls,
Haggard creatures though we be!

Racked and soiled the faded air
Freshens in our holiday;
Clouds and tides our respite share;
Breezes linger by the way.
Piper, rest! Piper, rest!
Now, a carol of the moon!
Piper, piper, play your best,
Melt the sun into your tune!

We are of the humblest grade;
Yet we dare to dance our fill:
Male and female were we made —
Fathers, mothers, lovers still!
Piper — softly; soft and low;
Pipe of love in mellow notes,
Till the tears begin to flow,
And our hearts are in our throats!

Nameless as the stars of night
Far in galaxies unfurled,
Yet we wield unrivalled might,
Joints and hinges of the world!
Night and day! night and day!
Sound the song the hours rehearse!
Work and play! work and play!
The order of the universe!

Now the furnaces are out,
And the aching anvils sleep;
Down the road a merry rout
Dances homeward twenty deep.

JUSTICE

▲

Piper, play! Piper, play!
Wearied people though we be,
Pipe for rest, pipe your best!
For a little we are free!

John Davidson

From St. George's Day

I cannot see the stars and flowers,
Nor hear the lark's soprano ring,
Because a ruddy darkness lowers
For ever, and the tempests sing.
I see the strong coerce the weak,
And labor overwrought rebel;
I hear the useless treadmill creak,
The prisoner, cursing in his cell;
I see the loafer-burnished wall;
I hear the rotting match-girl whine;
I see the unslept switchman fall;
I hear the explosion in the mine. . . .
I see along the heedless street
The sandwichmen trudge through the mire;
I hear the tired, quick-tripping feet
Of sad, gay girls who ply for hire.
The glowing blast, the fire-shot smoke
Where guns are forged and armor plate,
The mammoth hammer's pounding stroke,
The din of our dread iron date.

John Davidson

The Surf of the Slums

From the ominous vast of the city's deep,
The breast of the slumbrous, restless sea,

[37]

With a hushed and halting hunger creep
   The morning tides of humanity.

My heart grows dumb for the foaming strife
   Of the waking city's tidal flow,
For the violence of its lashing life
   And the weight of its deadly undertow.

                      Author Unknown

SLAVERY

Oh, for a lodge in some vast wilderness,
Some boundless contiguity of shade,
Where rumor of oppression and deceit,
Of unsuccessful or successful war,
Might never reach me more.   My ear is pained,
My soul is sick, with every day's report
Of wrong and outrage with which earth is filled.
There is no flesh in man's obdurate heart,
It does not feel for man; the natural bond
Of brotherhood is severed as the flax
That falls asunder at the touch of fire.

He finds his fellow guilty of a skin
Not colored like his own; and having power
To enforce the wrong, for such a worthy cause
Dooms and devotes him as his lawful prey.
Lands intersected by a narrow frith
Abhor each other.   Mountains interposed
Make enemies of nations, who had else
Like kindred drops been mingled into one.

Thus man devotes his brother, and destroys;
And, worse than all, and most to be deplored,

JUSTICE

As human nature's broadest, foulest blot,
Chains him, and tasks him, and exacts his sweat
With stripes, that Mercy, with a bleeding heart,
Weeps when she sees inflicted on a beast.

William Cowper

WEAVERS

Their eyelids are drooping, no tears lie beneath;
They stand at the loom and grind their teeth;
" We are weaving a shroud for the doubly dead,
And a threefold curse in its every thread —
    We are weaving, still weaving.

" A curse for the Godhead to whom we have bowed
In our cold and our hunger, we weave in the shroud;
For in vain have we hoped and in vain have we prayed;
He has mocked us and scoffed at us, sold and betrayed —
    We are weaving, still weaving.

" A curse for the king of the wealthy and proud,
Who for us had no pity, we weave in the shroud;
Who takes our last penny to swell out his purse,
While we die the death of a dog — yea, a curse —
    We are weaving, still weaving.

" A curse for our country, whose cowardly crowd
Hold her shame in high honor, we weave in the shroud;
Whose blossoms are blighted and slain in the germ,
Whose filth and corruption engender the worm —
    We are weaving, still weaving.

" To and fro flies our shuttle — no pause in its flight,
'Tis a shroud we are weaving by day and by night;

[39]

We are weaving a shroud for the worse than dead,
And a threefold curse in its every thread —
We are weaving — still weaving."

Heinrich Heine

THE TREAD OF THE POOR

Always the poor are with us,
Age-long is their tread.
Anxious or sodden their faces,
Weary and bent their forms,
Heavy, heavy their footsteps,
Shuffling over the earth.
When wild winds are shrieking
And the nights are black,
Do you not hear them shuffling,
Shuffling beneath your window,
Shuffling past your door?
Millions upon millions,
Poor, tired, patient feet,
Shuffling, shuffling, shuffling,
Can you not hear the shuffling,
Heavy tread of the poor?

Lee Spencer

POVERTY

The worst of ills, and hardest to endure,
Past hope, past cure,
Is Penury, who, with her sister-mate
Disorder, soon brings down the loftiest state,
And makes it desolate.

JUSTICE

This truth the sage of Sparta told,
    Aristodemus old —
" Wealth makes the man." On him that's poor
Proud Worth looks down, and Honor shuts the door.

Alcaeus
Greek poet, 611–580 B.C.

THE SAD SIGHT OF THE HUNGRY

'Twould please me, gods, if you would spare
Mine eyes from all this hungry stare
That fills the face and eyes of men
Who search for food o'er hill and glen.

Their eyes are orbs of dullest fire,
As if the flame would mount up higher;
But in the darkness of their glow
We know the fuel's burning low.

Such looks, O gods, are not from thee!
No, they're the stares of misery!
They speak of hunger's frightful hold
On lips a-dry and stomachs cold.

" Bread, bread," they cry, these weary men,
With wives and children from the glen!
Oh, they would toil the live-long day
But for a meal, their lives to stay.

But where is it in all the land?
Unless the gods with gen'rous hand
Send sweetsome rice and strength'ning corn
To these vast crowds to hunger born!

Li Hung Chang

[41]

The Sorrows of the World

I sit and look out upon all the sorrows of the world, and
    upon all oppression and shame,
I hear secret convulsive sobs from young men at anguish
    with themselves, remorseful after deeds done,
I see in low life the mother misused by her children,
    dying, neglected, gaunt, desperate,
I see the wife misused by her husband, I see the treach-
    erous seducer of young women,
I mark the ranklings of jealousy and unrequited love
    attempted to be hid, I see these sights on the earth,
I see the workings of battle, pestilence, tyranny, I see
    martyrs and prisoners,
I observe a famine at sea, I observe the sailors casting
    lots who shall be killed to preserve the lives of the
    rest,
I observe the slights and degradations cast by arrogant
    persons upon laborers, the poor, and upon negroes,
    and the like;
All these — all the meanness and agony without end I
    sitting look out upon,
See, hear, and am silent.

Walt Whitman

POEMS OF
JUSTICE

▲▲▲▲▲▲▲▲▲▲▲▲▲▲

THE MARCH OF
REVOLT

▼

LEGISLATORS

Woe unto them that decree unrighteous decrees, and
that write grievousness which they have prescribed;
to turn aside the needy from judgment, and to take
away the right from the poor of my people, that
widows may be their prey, and that they may rob
the fatherless!

And what will ye do in the day of visitation, and in the
desolation which shall come from far? to whom
will ye flee for help? and where will ye leave your
glory?

Isaiah
Hebrew prophet, 8th century, B.C.

"YOUR HANDS ARE FULL OF BLOOD"

Hear the word of the Lord, ye rulers of Sodom; give ear
unto the law of our God, ye people of Gomorrah.

To what purpose is the multitude of your sacrifices unto
me? saith the Lord. . . . Bring no more vain
oblations. . . .

When ye spread forth your hands, I will hide mine eyes
from you; yea when ye make many prayers I will
not hear; your hands are full of blood.

Isaiah
Hebrew prophet, 8th century, B.C.

[45]

JUSTICE

WALL STREET, 600 B.C.

They take up all of them with the angle, they catch them
in their net, and gather them in their drag; therefore they sacrifice unto their nets, and burn incense
unto their drags; because by them their portion is
fat, and their meat plenteous.

Habakkuk
Hebrew prophet, 6th century, B.C.

KINGS

Doth some one say that there be gods above?
There are not; no, there are not. Let no fool,
Led by the old false fable, thus deceive you.
Look at the facts themselves, yielding my words
No undue credence; for I say that kings
Kill, rob, break oaths, lay cities waste by fraud,
And doing thus are happier than those
Who live calm pious lives day after day.
How many little states that serve the gods
Are subject to the godless but more strong,
Made slaves by might of a superior army!

Euripides
Athenian poet, 5th century, B.C.

Translated by J. A. Symonds

PRIDE IN POVERTY

Riches and honor are what men desire; but if they attain
to them by improper ways, they should not con-
tinue to hold them.

[46]

Poverty and low estate are what men dislike; but if they are brought to such condition by improper ways, they should not feel shame for it.

Confucius
Chinese philosopher, 6th century, B.C.

SEEKING CAUSES

Neither drugs nor charms nor burnings will touch a deep-lying political sore any more than a bodily one; but only right and utter change of constitution;

And they do but lose their labor who think that by any tricks of law they can get the better of those mischiefs of commerce, and see not that they hew at a hydra.

Plato
Greek philosopher and poet, 4th century, B.C.

PALACES

Woe unto you who despise the humble dwelling and inheritance of your fathers!

Woe unto you who build palaces with the sweat of others!

Each stone, each brick of which it is built, is a sin!

The Book of Enoch

"GO TO NOW, YE RICH"

Go to now, ye rich men, weep and howl for your miseries that shall come upon you. Your riches are corrupted, and your garments are moth-eaten.

JUSTICE

Your gold and silver are cankered; and the rust of
them shall be a witness against you, and shall eat
your flesh as it were fire.

Ye have heaped treasures together for the last days.
Behold, the hire of the laborers who have reaped
down your fields, which is of you kept back by
fraud, crieth: and the cries of them which have
reaped are entered into the ears of the Lord of
Sabaoth.

Ye have lived in pleasure on the earth, and been wanton;
ye have nourished your hearts, as in a day of slaugh-
ter. Ye have condemned and killed the just: and he
doth not resist you.

Be patient, therefore, brethren, unto the coming of the
Lord. Behold, the husbandman waiteth for the
precious fruit of the earth, and hath long patience
for it, until he receive the early and latter rain. Be
ye also patient; stablish your hearts; for the coming
of the Lord draweth nigh.

The Epistle of James

JESUS

The martyred Christ of the working class, the inspired
evangel of the downtrodden masses, the world's supreme revolutionary leader,

Whose love for the poor and the children of the poor
hallowed all the days of His consecrated life, lighted
up and made forever holy the dark tragedy of His
death, and gave to the ages His divine inspiration
and His deathless name.

Eugene V. Debs

"How Far, O Rich"

How far, O rich, do you extend your senseless avarice?
  Do you intend to be the sole inhabitants of the
  earth? Why do you drive out the fellow sharers of
  nature, and claim it all for yourselves?
The earth was made for all, rich and poor, in common.
  Why do you rich claim it as your exclusive right?
  The soil was given to the rich and poor in common
  — wherefore, O ye rich, do you unjustly claim it
  for yourselves alone?
Nature gave all things in common for the use of all;
  usurpation created private rights.
Property hath no rights. The earth is the Lord's, and
  we are His offspring.
The pagans hold earth as property. They do blaspheme
  God.

Saint Ambrose

The Two Songs

I heard an Angel singing
When the day was springing:
" Mercy, pity, and peace,
Are the world's release."

So he sang all day
Over the new-mown hay,
Till the sun went down,
And haycocks looked brown.

I heard a Devil curse
Over the heath and the furze:
" Mercy could be no more
If there were nobody poor,

[49]

And pity no more could be
If all were happy as ye:
And mutual fear brings peace.
Misery's increase
Are mercy, pity, peace."

At his curse the sun went down,
And the heavens gave a frown.

William Blake

SONG TO THE MEN OF ENGLAND

Men of England, wherefore plow
For the lords who lay ye low?
Wherefore weave with toil and care
The rich robes your tyrants wear?

Wherefore feed and clothe and save,
From the cradle to the grave,
Those ungrateful drones who would
Drain your sweat — nay, drink your blood?

Wherefore, Bees of England, forge
Many a weapon, chain, and scourge,
That these stingless drones may spoil
The forced produce of your toil?

Have ye leisure, comfort, calm,
Shelter, food, love's gentle balm?
Or what is it ye buy so dear?
With your pain and with your fear?

The seed ye sow another reaps;
The wealth ye find another keeps;
The robes ye weave another wears;
The arms ye forge another bears.

Sow seed — but let no tyrant reap;
Find wealth — let no impostor heap;
Weave robes — let not the idle wear;
Forge arms — in your defence to bear.

Shrink to your cellars, holes, and cells;
In halls ye deck another dwells.
Why shake the chains ye wrought?   Ye see
The steel ye tempered glance on ye.

With plow and spade, and hoe and loom,
Trace your grave, and build your tomb,
And weave your winding-sheet, till fair
England be your sepulcher.

Percy Bysshe Shelley

WRITTEN IN LONDON, SEPTEMBER, 1802

O friend!   I know not which way I must look
For comfort, being, as I am, oppressed
To think that now our life is only dressed
For show; mean handy-work of craftsman, cook,
Or groom! — We must run glittering like a brook
In the open sunshine, or we are unblessed;
The wealthiest man among us is the best;
No grandeur now in nature or in book
Delights us.   Rapine, avarice, expense,
This is idolatry; and these we adore;
Plain living and high thinking are no more:
The homely beauty of the good old cause
Is gone; our peace, our fearful innocence,
And pure religion breathing household laws.

William Wordsworth

THE MASK OF ANARCHY

Men of England, Heirs of Glory,
Heroes of unwritten story,
Nurslings of one mighty mother,
Hopes of her, and one another!

Rise, like lions after slumber,
In unvanquishable number,
Shake your chains to earth like dew,
Which in sleep had fall'n on you.
Ye are many, they are few.

What is Freedom!   Ye can tell
That which Slavery is too well,
For its very name has grown
To an echo of your own.

'Tis to work, and have such pay
As just keeps life from day to day
In your limbs as in a cell
For the tyrants' use to dwell:

So that ye for them are made,
Loom, and plow, and sword, and spade;
With or without your own will, bent
To their defence and nourishment.

'Tis to see your children weak
With their mothers pine and peak,
When the winter winds are bleak —
They are dying whilst I spea˙

'Tis to hunger for such diet
As the rich man in his riot
Casts to the fat dogs that lie
Surfeiting beneath his eye.

[52]

▲

'Tis to be a slave in soul,
And to hold no strong control
Over your own wills, but be
All that others make of ye.

Percy Bysshe Shelley

THE MARSEILLAISE

Ye sons of toil, awake to glory!
  Hark, hark, what myriads bid you rise;
Your children, wives and grandsires hoary —
  Behold their tears and hear their cries!
Shall hateful tyrants, mischief breeding,
  With hireling hosts, a ruffian band —
  Affright and desolate the land,
While peace and liberty lie bleeding?

CHORUS

  To arms! to arms! ye brave!
    Th' avenging sword unsheathe!
  March on, march on, all hearts resolved
    On Victory or Death.

With luxury and pride surrounded,
  The vile, insatiate despots dare,
Their thirst for gold and power unbounded,
  To mete and vend the light and air;
Like beasts of burden would they load us,
  Like gods would bid their slaves adore,
  But Man is Man, and who is more?
Then shall they longer lash and goad us?   (Chorus)

O Liberty! can man resign thee,
  Once having felt thy generous flame?

Can dungeons' bolts and bars confine thee,
  Or whips thy noble spirit tame?
Too long the world has wept bewailing,
  That Falsehood's dagger tyrants wield;
  But Freedom is our sword and shield,
And all their arts are unavailing!   (Chorus)
            Claude Joseph Rouget de Lisle

WAT TYLER

" When Adam delved and Eve span,
Who was then the gentleman? "

Wretched is the infant's lot,
Born within the straw-roofed cot;
Be he generous, wise, or brave,
He must only be a slave.
Long, long labor, little rest,
Still to toil, to be oppressed;
Drained by taxes of his store,
Punished next for being poor:
This is the poor wretch's lot,
Born within the straw-roofed cot.

While the peasant works — to sleep,
What the peasant sows — to reap,
On the couch of ease to lie,
Rioting in revelry;
Be he villain, be he fool,
Still to hold despotic rule,
Trampling on his slaves with scorn!
This is to be nobly born.

" When Adam delved and Eve span,
Who was then the gentleman? "
            Robert Southey

The Internationale

Hymn of the revolutionary working-classes of all nations

Arise, ye prisoners of starvation!
   Arise, ye wretched of the earth,
For Justice thunders condemnation,
   A better world's in birth.
No more tradition's chains shall bind us,
   Arise, ye slaves! No more in thrall!
The earth shall rise on new foundations,
   We have been naught, we shall be all.

Refrain

   'Tis the final conflict,
      Let each stand in his place,
   The International Party
      Shall be the human race.

Behold them seated in their glory,
   The kings of mine and rail and soil!
What would you read in all their story
   But how they plundered toil?
Fruits of the people's work are buried
   In the strong coffers of a few;
In voting for their restitution
   The men will only ask their due.   (Refrain)

Toilers from shops and fields united,
   The party we of all who work;
The earth belongs to us, the people,
   No room here for the shirk.
How many on our flesh have fattened!
   But if the noisome birds of prey
Shall vanish from our sky some morning,
   The blessed sunlight still will stay.   (Refrain)

Eugene Pottier

▲

THE PEOPLE'S ANTHEM

When wilt Thou save the people?
  O God of mercy! when?
Not kings and lords, but nations!
  Not thrones and crowns, but men!
Flowers of Thy heart, O God, are they!
Let them not pass, like weeds, away!
Their heritage a sunless day!
      God save the people!

Shall crime bring crime for ever,
  Strength aiding still the strong?
Is it Thy will, O Father!
  That man shall toil for wrong?
" No! " say thy mountains; " No! " Thy skies;
" Man's clouded sun shall brightly rise,
And songs be heard instead of sighs."
      God save the people!

When wilt thou save the people?
  O God of mercy! when?
The people, Lord! the people!
  Not thrones and crowns, but men!
God save the people! Thine they are;
Thy children, as Thy angels fair;
Save them from bondage and despair!
      God save the people!

Ebenezer Elliott
" The Poet of the People "

SONG OF THE LOWER CLASSES

We plow and sow, we're so very, very low,
   That we delve in the dirty clay;
Till we bless the plain with the golden grain,
   And the vale with the fragrant hay.
Our place we know, we're so very, very low,
   'Tis down at the landlord's feet;
We're not too low the grain to grow,
   But too low the bread to eat.

Down, down we go, we're so very, very low,
   To the hell of the deep-sunk mines;
But we gather the proudest gems that glow,
   When the crown of the despot shines;
And when'er he lacks, upon our backs
   Fresh loads he deigns to lay;
We're far too low to vote the tax
   But not too low to pay.

We're low, we're low — we're very, very low —
   And yet from our fingers glide
The silken floss and the robes that glow
   Round the limbs of the sons of pride;
And what we get, and what we give,
   We know, and we know our share;
We're not too low the cloth to weave,
   But too low the cloth to wear.

We're low, we're low, we're very, very low,
   And yet when the trumpets ring,
The thrust of a poor man's arm will go
   Through the heart of the proudest king.

We're low, we're low — mere rabble, we know —
  We're only the rank and the file;
We're not too low to kill the foe,
  But too low to share the spoil.

Ernest Jones
Chartist leader

PEOPLE'S SONG, 1849

Weep, weep, weep and weep
  For pauper, dolt and slave!
Hark! from wasted moor and fen
Feverous alley, stifling den,
Swells the wail of Saxon men —
  Work! or the grave!

Down, down, down and down,
  With idler, knave, and tyrant!
Why for sluggards cark and moil?
He that will not live by toil
Has no right on English soil!
  God's word's our warrant!

Up, up, up and up!
  Face your game and play it!
The night is past, behold the sun!
The idols fall, the lie is done!
The Judge is set, the doom begun!
  Who shall stay it?

Charles Kingsley

▲

THE PARISH WORKHOUSE

Theirs is yon house that holds the village poor,
Whose walls of mud scarce bear the broken door —
There, where the putrid vapors flagging, play,
And the dull wheel hums doleful through the day.
There children dwell who know no parents' care;
Parents, who know no children's love, dwell there;
Heart-broken matrons on their joyless bed,
Forsaken wives and mothers never wed,
Dejected widows with unheeded tears,
And crippled age with more than childhood fears;
The lame, the blind, and, far the happiest they!
The moping idiot and the madman gay. . . .

Say ye, oppressed by some fantastic woes,
Some jarring nerve that baffles your repose;
Who press the downy couch, while slaves advance
With timid eye, to read the distant glance;
Who with sad prayers the weary doctor tease,
To name the nameless ever-new disease;
Who with mock patience dire complaints endure,
Which real pain and that alone can cure;
How would ye bear in real pain to lie,
Despised, neglected, left alone to die?
How would ye bear to draw your latest breath
Where all that's wretched pave the way for death?

George Crabbe

From " The Village "

THE VOICE OF TOIL

I heard men saying, Leave hope and praying,
All days shall be as all have been;
Today and tomorrow bring fear and sorrow,
The never-ending toil between.

When Earth was younger mid toil and hunger,
In hope we strove, and our hands were strong;
Then great men led us, with words they fed us,
And bade us right the earthly wrong.

Go read in story their deeds and glory,
Their names amidst the nameless dead:
Turn then from lying to us slow-dying
In that good world to which they led;

Where fast and faster our iron master,
The thing we made, forever drives,
Bids us grind treasure and fashion pleasure
For other hopes and other lives.

Where home is a hovel and dull we grovel,
Forgetting that the world is fair:
Where no babe we cherish, lest its very soul perish;
Where mirth is crime, and love a snare.

Who now shall lead us, what god shall heed us
As we lie in the hell our hands have won?
For us are no rulers but fools and befoolers:
The great are fallen, the wise men gone.

I heard men saying, Leave tears and praying,
The sharp knife heedeth not the sheep:
Are we not stronger than the rich and the wronger,
When day breaks over dreams and sleep?

JUSTICE

Come, shoulder to shoulder ere the world grows older!
Help lies in naught but thee and me:
Hope is before us, and the long years that bore us
Bore leaders more than men may be.

Let dead hearts tarry and trade and marry,
And trembling nurse their dreams of mirth,
While we the living our lives are giving
To bring the bright new world to birth.

Come, shoulder to shoulder ere earth grows older!
The Cause spreads over land and sea:
Now the world shaketh, and fear awaketh,
And joy at last for thee and me.

William Morris

THE REVOLUTION

Unhappy man! uplift thine eyes, look up to where a
thousand thousand gather on the hills in joyous expectation of the dawn!

Regard them, they are all thy brothers, sisters, the
troops of those poor wights who hitherto knew
naught of life but suffering, have been but strangers
on this earth of Joy; they all are waiting for that
Revolution which affrights thee, their redeemer
from this world of sorrow, creator of a new world
that blesses all!

See there, there stream the legions from the factories;
they have made and fashioned lordly stuffs —
themselves and children, they are naked, frozen,
hungry; for not to them belongs the fruit of all
their labor, but to the rich and mighty one who
calls men and the earth his own!

▲

So, there they troop, from fields and farmyards; they have tilled the earth and turned it to a smiling garden, and fruits in plenty, enough for all who live, have paid their pains — yet poor are they, and naked, starving; for not to them, nor to others who are needy, belongs earth's blessing, but solely to the rich and mighty one who calls men and the earth his own.

They all, the hundred-thousands, millions, are camped upon the hills and gaze into the distance, where thickening clouds proclaim the advent of emancipating Revolution; they all, to whom nothing is left to grieve for, from whom men rob the sons to train them into sturdy gaolers of their fathers; whose daughters walk the city's streets with burden of their shame, an offering to the baser lusts of rich and mighty; they all, with the sallow, careworn faces, the limbs devoured by frosts and hunger, they all who have never known joy, encamp there on the heights and strain their eyes in blissful expectation of its coming, and listen in rapt silence to the rustle of the rising storm, which fills their ears with Revolution's greeting.

Richard Wagner

THE MARCH OF THE WORKERS

What is this — the sound and rumor? What is this
    that all men hear,
Like the wind in hollow valleys when the storm is drawing near,
Like the rolling-on of ocean in the eventide of fear?
    'Tis the people marching on.

JUSTICE

Hark the rolling of the thunder!
Lo! the sun! and lo! thereunder
Riseth wrath, and hope, and wonder,
    And the host comes marching on.

Forth they come from grief and torment; on they go
    towards health and mirth.
All the wide world is their dwelling, every corner of the
    earth.
Buy them, sell them for thy service! Try the bargain
    what 'tis worth,
        For the days are marching on.   (Chorus)

Many a hundred years passed over have they labored
    deaf and blind;
Never tidings reached their sorrow, never hope their toil
    might find.
Now at last they've heard and hear it, and the cry comes
    down the wind
        And their feet are marching on.   (Chorus)

Is it war then? Will ye perish as the dry wood in the
    fire?
Is it peace? Then be ye of us, let your hope be our desire.
Come and live! for life awaketh, and the world shall
    never tire;
        And hope is marching on.   (Chorus)

William Morris

A Marching Song

We mix from many lands,
　　We march for very far;
In hearts and lips and hands
　　Our staffs and weapons are;
The light we walk in darkens sun and moon and star.

It doth not flame and wane
　　With years and spheres that roll,
Storm cannot shake nor strain
　　The strength that makes it whole,
The fire that molds and moves is of the sovereign
　　soul. . . .

From the edge of harsh derision,
　　From discord and defeat,
From doubt and lame division,
　　We pluck the fruit and eat;
And the mouth finds it bitter, and the spirit sweet. . . .

O nations undivided,
　　O single people and free,
We dreamers, we derided,
　　We mad blind men that see,
We bear you witness ere ye come that ye shall be.

Ye sitting among tombs,
　　Ye standing round the gate,
Whom fire-mouthed war consumes,
　　Or cold-lipped peace bids wait,
All tombs and bars shall open, every grave and
　　grate. . . .

O sorrowing hearts of slaves,
　　We heard you beat from far!

We bring the light that saves,
    We bring the morning star;
Freedom's good things we bring you, whence all good
    things are. . . .

    Rise, ere the dawn be risen;
      Come, and be all souls fed;
    From field and street and prison
      Come, for the feast is spread;
Live, for the truth is living; wake, for night is dead.

Algernon Charles Swinburne

From LES MISERABLES

Friends, the hour in which we live, and in which I speak
to you, is a gloomy hour, but of such is the terrible
price of the future. A revolution is a toll-gate.

Oh, the human race shall be delivered, uplifted and
consoled! We affirm it on this barricade. Whence
shall arise the shout of love, if it be not from the
summit of sacrifice?

O my brothers, here is the place of junction between
those who think and those who suffer; this barricade is made neither of paving-stones, nor of tim-
bers, nor of iron; it is made of two mounds, a
mound of ideas and a mound of sorrows.

Misery here encounters the ideal. Here day embraces
night, and says: I will die with thee and thou shalt
be born again with me.

From the pressure of all desolations, faith gushes forth.
Sufferings bring their agony here, and ideas their
immortality. This agony and this immortality are
to mingle and compose our death.

[65]

Brothers, he who dies here dies in the radiance of the future, and we are entering a grave illumined by the dawn.

Victor Hugo

From BOSTON HYMN

God said, " I am tired of kings,
 I suffer them no more;
Up to my ear the morning brings
 The outrage of the poor.

" My angel — his name is Freedom —
 Choose him to be your king;
He shall cut pathways east and west,
 And fend you with his wing.

" Lo! I uncover the land
 Which I hid of old time in the West,
As the sculptor uncovers the statue
 When he has wrought his best;

" I show Columbia, of the rocks
 Which dip their foot in the seas,
And soar to the air-borne flocks
 Of clouds, and the boreal fleece.

" I will divide my goods;
 Call in the wretch and slave:
None shall rule but the humble,
 And none but toil shall have.

" I will have never a noble,
 No lineage counted great;
Fishers and shoppers and plowmen
 Shall constitute a state.

▲

"Today unbind the captive:
    So only are ye unbound.
Lift up a people from the dust;
    Trump of their rescue, sound!

"Pay ransom to the owner,
    And fill the bag to the brim.
Who is the owner? The slave is owner,
    And ever was. Pay him!"

Ralph Waldo Emerson

THE ANTIQUITY OF FREEDOM

O Freedom! thou art not, as poets dream,
A fair young girl, with light and delicate limbs,
And wavy tresses gushing from the cap
With which the Roman master crowned his slave
When he took off the gyves. A bearded man,
Armed to the teeth, art thou; one mailed hand
Grasps the broad shield, and one the sword; thy brow,
Glorious in beauty though it be, is scarred
With tokens of old wars; thy massive limbs
Are strong with struggling. Power at thee has launched
His bolts, and with his lightnings smitten thee;
They could not quench the life thou hast from heaven.
Merciless Power has dug thy dungeon deep,
And his swart armorers, by a thousand fires,
Have forged thy chain; yet, while he deems thee bound,
The links are shivered, and the prison walls
Fall outward; terribly thou springest forth,
As springs the flame above a burning pile,
And shoutest to the nations, who return
Thy shoutings, while the pale oppressor flies.

William Cullen Bryant

[67]

From THE PRESENT CRISIS

When a deed is done for Freedom, through the broad
earth's aching breast
Runs a thrill of joy prophetic, trembling on from east
to west,
And the slave, where'er he cowers, feels the soul within
him climb
To the awful verge of manhood, as the energy sublime
Of a century bursts full-blossomed on the thorny stem
of Time.

Careless seems the great Avenger: history's pages but
record
One death-grapple in the darkness 'twixt old systems
and the Word;
Truth forever on the scaffold, Wrong forever on the
throne, —
Yet that scaffold sways the future, and, behind the dim
unknown,
Standeth God within the shadow, keeping watch above
His own.

Once to every man and nation comes the moment to
decide;
In the strife of Truth with Falsehood, for the good or
evil side,
Some great cause, God's new Messiah, offering each the
bloom or blight,
Parts the goats upon the left hand and the sheep upon
the right,
And the choice goes by forever 'twixt that darkness and
that light.

For humanity sweeps onward: where today the martyr
stands,

On the morrow crouches Judas with the silver in his
    hands;
Far in front the cross stands ready and the crackling
    fagots burn,
While the hooting mob of yesterday in silent awe return
To glean up the scattered ashes into History's golden
    urn.

New occasions teach new duties; Time makes ancient
    good uncouth;
They must upward still, and onward, who would keep
    abreast of Truth;
Lo, before us gleam her camp-fires! we ourselves must
    Pilgrims be,
Launch our Mayflower, and steer boldly through the
    desperate winter sea,
Nor attempt the Future's portal with the Past's blood-
    rusted key.

James Russell Lowell

THE MAN WITH THE HOE *

*God made man in his own image:
in the image of God He made him. — Genesis.*

Bowed by the weight of centuries he leans
Upon his hoe and gazes on the ground,
The emptiness of ages in his face,
And on his back the burden of the world.
Who made him dead to rapture and despair,
A thing that grieves not and that never hopes,
Stolid and stunned, a brother to the ox?
Who loosened and let down this brutal jaw?

* Written after seeing Millet's world-famous painting of a
brutalized toiler in the deep abyss of labor.

Whose was the hand that slanted back this brow?
Whose breath blew out the light within this brain?

Is this the Thing the Lord God made and gave
To have dominion over sea and land;
To trace the stars and search the heavens for power;
To feel the passion of Eternity?
Is this the dream He dreamed who shaped the suns
And marked their ways upon the ancient deep?
Down all the caverns of Hell to their last gulf
There is no shape more terrible than this —
More tongued with cries against the world's blind
    greed —
More filled with signs and portents for the soul —
More packed with danger to the universe.

What gulfs between him and the seraphim!
Slave of the wheel of labor, what to him
Are Plato and the swing of Pleiades?
What the long reaches of the peaks of song,
The rift of dawn, the reddening of the rose?
Through this dread shape the suffering ages look;
Time's tragedy is in that aching stoop;
Through this dread shape humanity betrayed,
Plundered, profaned and disinherited,
Cries protest to the Powers that made the world,
A protest that is also prophecy.

O masters, lords and rulers in all lands,
Is this the handiwork you give to God,
This monstrous thing distorted and soul-quenched?
How will you ever straighten up this shape;
Touch it again with immortality;
Give back the upward looking and the light;

Rebuild in it the music and the dream;
Make right the immemorial infamies,
Perfidious wrongs, immedicable woes?

O masters, lords and rulers in all lands,
How will the future reckon with this Man?
How answer his brute question in that hour
When whirlwinds of rebellion shake all shores?
How will it be with kingdoms and with kings —
With those who shaped him to the thing he is —
When this dumb Terror shall rise to judge the world,
After the silence of the centuries?

Edwin Markham

THE MAMMON MONSTER

I see a monster.
His feet are of gold; his hands are of gold;
Golden is his head and his legs are golden.
His heart is of clay.
His greedy hands are folded upon
His swollen belly.
Into his maw flows an endless procession:
Men with gray faces, women with sunken eyes,
And the little children who have never laughed.

Charles Erskine Scott Wood

From NINEVEH

O Nineveh, thy realm is set
   Upon a base of rock and steel
From where the under-rivers fret
   High up to where the planets reel.

Clad in a blazing coat of mail,
  Above the gables of the town
Huge dragons with a monstrous trail
  Have pillared pathways up and down.

And in the bowels of the deep
  Where no man sees the gladdening sun,
All night without the balm of sleep
  The human tide rolls on and on.

. . . . .

The Hudson's mighty waters lave
  In stern caress thy granite shore,
And to thy port the salt sea wave
  Brings oil and wine and precious ore.

Yet if the ocean in its might
  Should rise confounding stream and bay,
The stain of one delirious night
  Not all the tides can wash away.

. . . . .

Thick pours the smoke of thousand fires,
  Life throbs and beats relentlessly —
But lo, above the stately spires
  Two lemans: Death and Leprosy.

What fruit shall spring from such embrace?
  Ah, even thou wouldst quake to hear!
He bends to kiss her loathsome face,
  She laughs — and whispers in his ear.

Sit not too proudly on thy throne,
  Think on thy sisters, them that fell;
Not all the hosts of Babylon
  Could save her from the jaws of hell.

George Sylvester Viereck

[72]

The March of the Hungry Men

In the dreams of your downy couches,
   Through the shades of your pampered sleep,
Give ear, you can hear it coming,
   The tide that is steady and deep —
Give ear, for the sound is growing,
   From desert and dungeon and den;
The tramp of the hungry millions,
   The march of the Hungry Men.

    .   .   .   .   .

So comes another army,
   Your wit cannot compute,
The man-at-arms self-fashioned,
   The man you made the brute,
From the farm and sweatshop gathered,
   From factory, mine and mill,
With lyre and shears and augur,
   Dibble and drift and drill.

They bear no sword nor rifle,
   Yet their ladders are on your walls.
Though the hauberk is turned to a jumper,
   The jambreaux to overalls;
They come from locomotive,
   From cab and cobbler's bench;
They are armed with the pick and the jackplane,
   The sledge and the ax and the wrench.

And some come empty handed,
   With fingers gnarled and strong,
And some come dumb with sorrow,
   And some come drunk with song;

But all that you thought were buried
  Are stirring and lithe and quick.
And they carry a brass-bound scepter:
  The brass composing-stick.

Through the depths of the Devil's darkness,
  With the distant stars for light,
They are coming, the while you slumber,
  And they come with the might of Right.
On a morrow — perhaps tomorrow —
  You will waken and see, and then
You will hand the keys of the cities
  To the ranks of the Hungry Men.

Author Unknown

THE TOILER: THE HOE-MAN OF THE AGES

*Companion piece to "The Thinker," written after
seeing Rodin's statue, "The Thinker," the
brutalized toiler.*

I

What strange awakening shape is this —
What is his breed, his genesis?
Peer into the past: from every age
His visage stares in silent rage.
Down the long centuries he came . . .
Who is he? Ask the sands his name.
Who is he? Ask the leaves that die,
And have no language but a sigh.
Ask the gray fields he plowed for bread
To feed the nations — he, unfed.
Ask the slow vultures as they wheel
Over the battles for a meal.

II

Behold, he is the Toiling Man,
Unresting since the world began.
What blind road has he come to this —
Out of what darkness, what abyss?
Grinding grim blocks in ages gone,
His groans gave Greece the Parthenon:
Out of the deeps of his despair,
The Colosseum whirled in air.
Back somewhere in the night of years,
The bricks of Babel felt his tears.
Back in the ages, stooped with loads,
Silent to curses and to goads,
With panting mouth and sullen lids,
He piled the monstrous Pyramids.
Yea, staggering under stripes and scars,
He heaved huge Cheops to the stars.
The Memphian Sphinxes in their day
Saw him go by as still as they.
And on all roads he ever trod
His silence was his cry to God.

He built and beautified the cities —
Gardens where rhymers thrummed their ditties;
Mansions where lolled the idling host,
Whose god is he that idles most;
Temples where pontiffs lit a flame
To gods that winked at all the shame.
His brute hands lifted into air
Bright Babylon, and held her there.
Yea, out of grief and reeking grime,
He lifted cities into Time —
Lifted their mighty splendors high,
And held them glittering in the sky.

III

So in those hands he held the fate
Of empires — carried their doom and date —
The power to wreck the guarded thrones
And leave the world a plain of stones.
Yea, there was strength in that huge girth
To flatten out the belly of earth:
In those bowed shoulders was the might
To draw down whirlwind and the night.
Yet he toiled humbly in all lands,
The fate of nations in his hands —
Toiled at his all-bestowing task,
And why he toiled he did not ask.
He let the centuries go by
Without a word, without a cry.
The stones were silent on the way,
And he groped on as still as they.

IV

Behold, O world, the Toiling Man,
Bearing earth's burden and her ban.
Because of his all-giving grace,
Kaisers and kings have held their place —
Because he gave ungrudging toil,
The Lords have had the world for spoil —
Because he gave them all his dower,
Great ladies glittered out their hour.
He clothed these paupers, gave them bed,
Put into their mouths their daily bread.
And his reward? A crust to taste,
An unknown grave upon the waste.
Outcast and cursed, befooled and flayed,
With earth's brute burdens on him laid,

▲

He only reached out humble hands,
Reached out his mercies on all lands.
How silent down the world he trod —
How patient he has been with God!

Edwin Markham

From THE TITAN

Loose him and let him go!
Ye men of privilege, ye men of power!
The giant who has risen in this hour,
Bearing a crown of sweat upon his brow —
His name is Labor and his time is *Now.*
Think you Tradition's womb can hold him long?
Progress is with him and his arm is strong.
And feel ye not the passion of his throe?
How dare ye then to bind him to his woe?
Loose him and let him go!

His feet are set in centuries of soil,
His mighty arms about the earth are furled,
Upon his brow the diadem of toil —
His sinews are the courage of the world.
Loose him and let him go!   His time is come.
Without him forge and factory were dumb.
But for his hand the soil would not give birth —
All fires go back upon the nation's hearth.
There is no labor where he has no part,
Commerce keeps time to his tremendous heart;
Tunnels, and towers, battleships and mines,
The plenteous products of the fields and vines,
The teeming industry of all the land
He holds within the hollow of his hand.
Cities and parks and palaces and mills —
  These are his works to do with as he wills.

Lo, from his eyes look forth the eyes of God!
Yea, from his eyes the eyes of God look out!
The voice of God is heard within his shout!

Angela Morgan

WOMEN

They looked from farmhouse windows;
Their joyless faces showed
Between the curtain and the sill —
You saw them from the road.
They looked up while they churned and cooked
And washed and swept and sewed.
Some could die and some just lived and many a one went
    mad.
But it's " Mother, be up at four o'clock," the men-folk
    bade.

They looked from town-house windows,
A shadow on the shade
Rose-touched by colorful depths of room
Where harmonies were made.
Within, the women went and came
And delicately played.
Some could grow and some could work, but many of
    them were dead.
" We must be gowned and gay tonight when the men
    come home," they said.

They looked from factory windows
Where many an iron gin
Drew in their days and ground their days
On the black wheels within,

Drew in their days and wove their days
To a web exceeding thin.
And they suffered what women have suffered over and
over again.
And it's "Double your speed for a living wage, ye
mothers and wives of men!"

They looked from brothel windows
And caught the curtain down.
A piteous, beckoning hand thrust out
To summon or clod or clown.
They named them true, they named them true,
The Women of the Town.
Some could live and some just died and most of them
none of us know.
And it's "What if the fallen women vote!" from the
men who keep them so.

Faint from without the windows
In many a fallow land
There sounds a trample of feet, and a light
Is flashed from hand to hand.
And out of the dark grow a frightened few
Who dimly understand.
Some are wise and some are less and many more are in
doubt.
But it's "This is death! And there lies life? We charge
you to find it out!"

What is the news from the windows now?
At some the faces throng
And the cries: "Come soon or we wait in vain,
We who have waited long."
From some a curious glance is flung
With the bars of a careless song.

Some are open and some are closed and some are hung
    for a feast,
And some stare blank as a harem wall curtained against
    the east.

Dear God, to watch the women look!
From task and game they turn,
Some are afraid of losing men
And some of what they earn,
Some light the sacrificial flame
And dare not watch it burn.
Some are scornful, some bar the door at the sound of the
    first alarms,
But it's " Mother, beware! It is we you chain! " And
    the babes leap in their arms.

All swift the cry comes down the world:
" Take task and take caress,
But, by our living spirits, we
Have other ways to bless.
Now let us teach the thing we've learned
In labor and loneliness.
We strive with none. We fold men home by the power
    of a great new word.
We who have long been dead are alive. We too are Thy
    people, Lord! "

Zona Gale

BUSINESS

All of the boxes and cartons of glass,
All the enamel and porcelain ware,
And even four-thousand pound intricate, delicate pieces
    of machinery
Are placarded
      Handle with Care

But the hands and feet of the truckers,
And the hearts and hopes of the truckers,
And the lives and souls of the truckers,
These are not placarded
Handle with Care.

Charles Grenville Hamilton

THE MAN UNDER THE STONE

When I see a workingman with mouths to feed,
Up, day after day, in the dark before the dawn,
And coming home, night after night, through the dusk,
Swinging forward like some fierce silent animal,
I see a man doomed to roll a huge stone up an endless
    steep.
He strains it onward inch by stubborn inch,
Crouched always in the shadow of the rock. . . .
See where he crouches, twisted, cramped, misshapen!
    He lifts for *their* life:
    The veins knot and darken —
    Blood surges into his face. . . .
    Now he loses — now he wins —
    Now he loses — loses — (God of my soul!)
    He digs his feet into the earth —
    There's a movement of terrified effort. . . .
    It stirs — it moves!
    Will the huge stone break his hold
    And crush him as it plunges to the Gulf?

The silent struggle goes on and on,
Like two contending in a dream.

Edwin Markham

[81]

Heirs of Time

From street and square, from hill and glen,
  Of this vast world beyond my door,
I hear the tread of marching men,
  The patient armies of the poor.

Not ermine-clad or clothed in state,
  Their title-deeds not yet made plain,
But waking early, toiling late,
  The heirs of all the earth remain.

The peasant brain shall yet be wise,
  The untamed pulse grow calm and still;
The blind shall see, the lowly rise,
  And work in peace Time's wondrous will.

Some day, without a trumpet's call
  This news will o'er the world be blown:
" The heritage comes back to all;
  The myriad monarchs take their own."

Thomas Wentworth Higginson

Trade

O trade! O trade! would thou wert dead!
The time needs heart — 'tis tired of head.

. . . . .

Grant thee, O trade, thine uttermost hope:
Level red gold with blue sky-slope,
And base it deep as devils grope:
When all's done, what hast thou won
Of the only sweet that's under the sun?
Ay, canst thou buy a single sigh
Of true love's least, least ecstasy?

[82]

▲

·   ·   ·   ·   ·

Who said once, in the lordly tone,
Man shall not live by bread alone,
But by all that cometh from the throne?

·   ·   ·   ·   ·

Love alone can do.
And ever love hears the women's sighing,
And ever hears sweet knighthood's defying,
And ever wise childhood's deep implying,
But never a trader's glozing and lying.

Sidney Lanier

From " The Symphony "

GOD AND THE STRONG ONES

" We have made them fools and weak! " said the Strong
Ones:
  " We have bound them, they are dumb and deaf and
blind;
We have crushed them in our hands like a heap of crum-
bling sands,
  We have left them naught to seek or find:
They are quiet at our feet! " said the Strong Ones;
  " We have made them one with wood and stone and
clod;
Serf and laborer and woman, they are less than wise or
human! — "
  " *I shall raise the weak!* " *saith God.*

" They are stirring in the dark! " said the Strong Ones,
  " They are struggling, who were moveless like the
dead·

[83]

JUSTICE

▲

We can hear them cry and strain hand and foot against
    the chain,
  We can hear their heavy upward tread. . . .
What if they are restless? " said the Strong Ones;
  " What if they have stirred beneath the rod?
Fools and weak and blinded men, we can tread them
    down again — "
  " Shall ye conquer Me? " saith God.

" They will trample us and bind! " said the Strong Ones;
  " We are crushed beneath the blackened feet and
    hands;
All the strong and fair and great they will crush from
    out the state;
  They will whelm it with the weight of pressing
    sands —
They are maddened and are blind! " said the Strong
    Ones;
  " Black decay has come where they have trod;
They will break the world in twain if their hands are on
    the rein — "
  " What is that to Me? " saith God.

*" Ye have made them in their strength, who were Strong
    Ones,*
  Ye have only taught the blackness ye have known:
*These are evil men and blind? — Ay, but molded to
    your mind!*
  How shall ye cry out against your own?
Ye have held the light and beauty I have given
  Far above the muddied ways where they must plod:
*Ye have builded this your lord with the lash and with
    the sword —*
  Reap what ye have sown! " saith God.

*ir*garet Widdemer

[84]

To Labor

Shall you complain who feed the world?
Who clothe the world?
Who house the world?
Shall you complain who are the world,
Of what the world may do?
As from this hour
You use your power,
The world must follow you!

The world's life hangs on your right hand!
Your strong right hand,
Your skilled right hand,
You hold the whole world in your hand,
See to it what you do!
Or dark or light,
Or wrong or right,
The world is made by you!

Then rise as you never rose before!
Nor hoped before!
Nor dared before!
And show as was never shown before,
The power that lies in you!
Stand all as one!
See justice done!
Believe, and Dare, and Do!

Charlotte Perkins Gilman

A Song of Labor

I have builded your towns and cities,
And over your widest streams
I have flung with a giant's ardor
The web of strong steel beams.

[85]

I have carved out the busy highways
　That mark where your commerce reigns;
With hammer and forge and anvil
　I have wrought your golden gains.

I have girded rock-ribbed mountains
　With rails for the iron steed;
I have delved in the old earth's bosom
　To answer the great world's greed,
I have clothed you, housed you, fed you,
　For thousands of years gone by;
I have stepped to the front when duty
　Has called, and I've answered "I! "

I have wrung from the soil denied me
　Your toll of the golden grains;
I have garbed you in silks and satins —
　And fettered my limbs with chains.
I have given my sweat and muscle
　To build for you, stone on stone,
The palace of ease and pleasure —
　The hut I may call my own.

For a thousand years you've driven —
　A thousand years and a day,
But I, like another Samson,
　Am giving my muscles play.
My brain is no longer idle;
　I see with a clearer sight,
And, piercing the gloom about me,
　I'm seeing, thank God, the light!

I see in the days before me
　My share of the things I've wrought;
See Justice no longer blinded —
　The weights of her scales unbought.

I see in the not far future
  The day when the worker's share
Is more than his belly's succor;
  Is more than a rag to wear.

I see on the morrow's mountains
  The glints of a golden dawn;
The dawn of a day fast coming
  When strivings and hates are gone.
Lo, out of the vasty darkness
  That fetters my limbs like steel
I can hear the swelling chorus
  That sings of the common weal.

Will M. Maupin

THE WEAK

We were born of night and terror in a wilderness of fear.

We were made to be your burdens till your tyrants disappear.

Hatred, greed, despair, for ages were our grandams and our sires:

We were mangled in the mountains, ringed around with frosts and fires.

Starving men begat in horror our forerunners weak as we.

Sickly mothers gave us suck. We lost our brothers in the sea.

We were seized and we were shaken by a million mouths of pain.

We were trapped and we were taken, and in torment we were slain.

We were slaves to lusts that slew us slowly. We were slaves to toil.

Chain gangs marched across the meadows. Rotting figs
and rancid oil
Were our rations. We went naked in the galleys, in the
sun.
We were slaves to lies that slew us slowly, surely, one
by one.

Little children in your mills, and babies butchered in
your streets,
Men in mines you doom to darkness; women, life's last
vile defeats,
Lawyers, liars, scribes and teachers who a nation's soul
betray;
Perjured priests and healers, slowly stumbling toward
the light of day.

So we have defiled for ages out of darkness. Now we see
New salvation made for millions, nearer. So our
thoughts go free.
Year by year you cure our bodies; teach our rotting
souls to know
Well, that mind shall make immortal, life's last fear
shall overthrow.
We were weak to make you stronger. Like your children
we shall grow.

John Curtis Underwood

THE BITTER CRY OF THE CHILDREN

Do ye hear the children weeping, O my brothers,
  Ere the sorrow comes with years?
They are leaning their young heads against their
    mothers —
  And *that* cannot stop their tears.

JUSTICE

The young lambs are bleating in the meadows;
   The young birds are chirping in the nest;
The young fawns are playing with the shadows;
   The young flowers are blowing toward the west—
But the young, young children, O my brothers,
   They are weeping bitterly!
They are weeping in the playtime of the others,
   In the country of the free.

Do you question the young children in the sorrow
   Why their tears are falling so?
The old man may weep for his tomorrow
   Which is lost in Long Ago;
The old tree is leafless in the forest,
   The old year is ending in the frost,
The old wound, if stricken, is the sorest,
   The old hope is hardest to be lost:
But the young, young children, O my brothers,
   Do you ask them why they stand
Weeping sore before the bosoms of their mothers,
   In our happy Fatherland?

They look up with their pale and sunken faces,
   And their looks are sad to see,
For the man's hoary anguish draws and presses
   Down the cheeks of infancy;
" Your old earth," they say, " is very dreary,
   Our young feet," they say, " are very weak;
Few paces have we taken, yet are weary —
   Our grave-rest is very far to seek.
Ask the old why they weep, and not the children,
   For the outside earth is cold,
And we young ones stand without, in our bewildering,
   And the graves are for the old." . . .

▲

"For oh," say the children, "we are weary,
 And we cannot run or leap;
If we cared for any meadows, it were merely
 To drop down in them and sleep.
Our knees tremble sorely in the stooping,
 We fall upon our faces, trying to go;
And, underneath our heavy eyelids drooping,
 The reddest flower would look as pale as snow.
For, all day, we drag our burden tiring
 Through the coal-dark, underground,
Or, all day, we drive the wheels of iron
 In the factories, round and round.

"For, all day, the wheels are droning, turning;
 Their wind comes in our faces,
Till our hearts turn, our head, with pulses burning,
 And the walls turn in their places:
Turns the sky in the high window blank and reeling,
 Turns the long light that drops adown the wall,
Turn the black flies that crawl along the ceiling,
 All are turning, all the day, and we with all.
And all day, the iron wheels are droning,
 And sometimes we could pray,
'O ye wheels,' (breaking out in a mad moaning)
 'Stop! be silent for today!'" . . .

They look up, with their pale and sunken faces,
 And their look is dread to see,
For they mind you of the angels in their places,
 With eyes turned on Deity.
"How long," they say, "how long, O cruel nation,
 Will you stand, to move the world, on a child's heart,
Stifle down with a mailed heel its palpitation,
 And tread onward to your throne amid the mart?

▲

Our blood splashes upward, O gold-heaper,
   And your purple shows your path!
But the child's sob in the silence curses deeper
   Than the strong man in his wrath."

Elizabeth Barrett Browning

The Children of the Poor

Take heed of this small child of earth;
   He is great; he hath in him God most high.
Children before their fleshly birth
   Are lights alive in the blue sky.

In our light, bitter world of wrong
   They come; God gives us them awhile.
His speech is in their stammering tongue,
   And His forgiveness in their smile.

Their sweet light rests upon our eyes.
   Alas! their right to joy is plain.
If they are hungry, Paradise
   Weeps, and, if cold, Heaven thrills with pain.

The want that saps their sinless flower
   Speaks judgment on sin's ministers.
Man holds an angel in his power.
   Ah! deep in Heaven what thunder stirs,

When God seeks out these tender things
   Whom in the shadow where we sleep
He sends us clothed about with wings,
   And finds them ragged babes that weep!

Victor Hugo

Translated from the French by A. C. Swinburne

CHILDREN OF TOIL

Ah, who are these on whom the vital bloom
Of life has withered to the dust of doom?
These little pilgrims prematurely worn
And bent as if they bore the weight of years?
These childish faces, pallid and forlorn,
Too dull for laughter and too hard for tears?
Is this the ghost of that insane crusade
That led ten thousand children long ago,
A flock of innocents, deceived, betrayed,
Yet pressing on through want and woe
To meet their fate, faithful and unafraid?
Nay, for a million children now
Are marching in the long, pathetic line,
With weary step and early wrinkled brow;
And at their head appears no holy sign
Of hope in heaven;
For unto them is given
No cross to carry, but a cross to drag.
Before their strength is ripe they bear
The load of labor, toiling underground,
In dangerous mines and breathing heavy air
Of crowded shops; their tender lives are bound
To service of the whirling clattering wheels
That fill the factories with dust and noise;
They are not girls and boys,
But little " hands " who blindly, dumbly feed
With their own blood the hungry god of Greed.

Henry van Dyke

From " Who Follow the Flag "

THE PRICE OF SUGAR

A summer under open skies,
A child — a thousand children,
A burning sun, cold rains
— And sugar beets.
A summer working sugar beets,
And youth — youth pulled and topped
And plowed beneath the soil
— As fertilizer.
Youth pulled and topped, and granulated,
And weighed — weighed out in bags
For us to buy, and please
Our tooth for sweets.
A summer under open skies,
A child — a future forming;
No schooling to distract
From sugar beets.

Frances B. Williams

THE LEADEN-EYED

Let not young souls be smothered out before
They do quaint deeds and fully flaunt their pride.
It is the world's one crime its babes grow dull,
Its poor are ox-like, limp and leaden-eyed.

Not that they starve, but starve so dreamlessly,
Not that they sow, but that they seldom reap,
Not that they serve, but have no gods to serve,
Not that they die, but that they die like sheep.

Vachel Lindsay

The Prop

This twig —
All bent and broken.

A beanstalk falls —
A stake of wood
Is needed to support it.
Impatient hands
Tear off this verdant twig
And set it to the task.

A wind, a rain.
The twig,
Snatched from the source
That nourished it and gave it growth,
Weakens — bends — gives way.
Its fiber bears but ill
The heavy beanstalk's weight.

Displace it now.
— A new one.
Easy done.

Unheeding hands
Toss it aside.
Oblivion.
— What matter that?
There are so many twigs.

Frances B. Williams

The Flower Factory

Lizabetta, Marianina, Fiametta, Teresina,
They are winding stems of roses, one by one, one by one,
Little children who have never learned to play;

▲

Teresina softly crying that her fingers ache today;
Tiny Fiametta nodding, when the twilight slips in, gray.
High above the clattering street, ambulance and fire-
    gong beat,
They sit, curling crimson petals, one by one, one by one.

Lizabetta, Marianina, Fiametta, Teresina,
They have never seen a rose-bush nor a dew-drop in the
    sun.
They will dream of the vendetta, Teresina, Fiametta,
Of a Black Hand and a Face behind a grating;
They will dream of cotton petals, endless, crimson,
    suffocating,
Never of a wild rose thicket or the singing of a cricket,
But the ambulance will bellow through the wanness of
    their dreams,
And their tired lids will flutter with the street's hysteric
    screams.

Lizabetta, Marianina, Fiametta, Teresina,
They are winding stems of roses, one by one, one by one.
Let them have a long, long playtime, Lord of Toil,
    when toil is done,
Fill their baby hands with roses, joyous roses of the sun.

Florence Wilkinson Evans

CHILD LABOR

No fledgling feeds the father bird!
    No chicken feeds the hen!
No kitten mouses for the cat —
    This glory is for men:

▲

We are the Wisest, Strongest Race —
Loud may our praise be sung!
The only animal alive
That lives upon its young!

Charlotte Perkins Gilman

THE GOLF LINKS LIE SO NEAR THE MILL

The golf links lie so near the mill
That almost every day
The laboring children can look out
And see the men at play.

Sarah N. Cleghorn

THE EASTER CHILDREN

" Christ the Lord is risen! "
Chant the Easter children,
Their love-molded faces
Luminous with gladness,
And their costly raiment
Gleaming like the lilies.

But last night I wandered
Where Christ had not risen,
Where love knows no gladness,
Where the lord of Hunger
Leaves no room for lilies,
And no time for childhood.

And today I wonder
Whether I am dreaming;
For above the swelling
Of their Easter music
I can hear the murmur,
" Suffer *all* the children."

▲

Nay, the world is dreaming!
And my seeing spirit
Trembles for its waking,
When their Savior rises
To restore the lilies
To the outcast children.

Elsa Barker

OUR TRADE

We have given our days to iron and steel
In dirt and danger for little pay,
Standing in front of a grinder wheel,
A screw machine, or a lathe all day.

Except for some hours in the twilight gray,
And an hour at noon for a smoke and a meal,
We have given our days to iron and steel
In dirt and danger for little pay.

Of a warm blue sky and the wind's soft steal
Over the prairie and through the hay,
What can we know or what can we feel,
We in the shop who can only say,
We have given our days to iron and steel?

Robert Gates

THE CHEATED CHILD

" I was born into this world with a chance to be happy,
   healthy and honest.
I opened my eyes into a world that needed me.
But — my mind is slow, my eyes weak, my nerves raw,
   my body twisted.

[97]

I meet life with doubts and fears (too weak to make a
     winning fight),
I — I who was born to work and laugh and play.
I am sixty-five per cent of the children of my country.
Dear God, I am the future of my race,
I am the cheated child."

Author Unknown

They Will Say

Of my city the worst that men will ever say is this:
You took little children away from the sun and the dew,
And the glimmers that played in the grass under the
     great sky,
And the reckless rain; you put them between walls
To work, broken and smothered, for bread and wages,
To eat dust in their throats and die empty-hearted
For a little handful of pay on a few Saturday nights.

Carl Sandburg

The Working Children to the Story Teller

Tell us a story to make us see
Things that gleamed on us long ago;
   Daisy meadows and fairy rings,
    Greening woods, where the brown thrush sings,
    And the shining blue where a sea gull wings,
      Teller of tales!

Tell us a story to make us hear
Murmurs we dreamed ere we were born;
   Rippling water and running breeze,
    Bobolink's note in the windy trees,
    And the mighty silence of summer seas;
      Teller of tales!

Tell us a story to make us feel
Childhood's blood in our veins again.
   For we are tired of grown-up fears,
   Tired of grown-up pains and tears,
   Sick of the stretch of the sordid years,
Give us a chance to laugh again,
Give us a play hour in our pain,
      Teller of tales!

Laura Benét

A GIRL STRIKE-LEADER

A white-faced, stubborn little thing
   Whose years are not quite twenty years,
   Eyes steely now and done with tears,
Mouth scornful of its suffering —

The young mouth! — body virginal
   Beneath the cheap, ill-fitting suit,
   A bearing quaintly resolute,
A flowering hat, satirical.

A soul that steps to the sound of the fife
   And banners waving red to war,
   Mystical, knowing scarce wherefore —
A Joan in a modern strife.

Florence Kiper Frank

PRAYER OF THE POOR

Written in a Chicago park

For the joy of cool, green places,
For the smiles of kindly faces,
   We, the poor, give thanks today;
We, the care-beridden moilers,

We, the broken, prisoned toilers
  Would not, thankless, go our way.

But we want the scent of roses
For our joy, when each day closes,
  Lest our drudging starve our souls;
For our children give us flowers,
Give us rest and laughing hours,
  Give us homes and hearths as goals.

We would work, but not with sighing;
We would build, but not by dying—
  We are not dumb brutes, but men!
For our errors grant us pardon,
But, O Lord, let Eden's garden
  With its beauty come again!

Thomas Curtis Clark

How?

How do they live who never see the sky
Save some gray patch by noon,
All smeared with dirty smoke?
Housed in foul tenements, reared in vile stench,
Broken by drudgery, hopeless through life,
  How do they live?

How can they live who never turn their hands
To any useful work,
Yet know their ease is fed
By ceaseless toil and misery?
That other human beings die too soon
That they may live in luxury?
  How can they live?

Lee Spencer

[100]

JUSTICE

▲

MAN AS GOD

How vain! he cried. A God? a mole, a worm!
An engine frail, of brittle bones conjoined;
With tissue packed; with nerves, transmitting force;
And driven by water, thick and colored red:
That may for some few pence a day be hired
In thousands to be shot at! Oh, a God
That lies and steals and murders!   Such a God
Passionate, dissolute, incontinent!
A God that starves in thousands, and ashamed,
In mines and foundries!   An enchanted God,
Whose nostrils in a palace breathe perfume,
Whose cracking shoulders hold the palace up,
Whose shoeless feet are rotting in the mire!

John Davidson

From " A Ballad in Blank Verse "

From THE BALLAD OF READING GAOL

I know not whether Laws be right,
    Or whether Laws be wrong;
All that we know who lie in jail
    Is that the wall is strong;
And that each day is like a year,
    A year whose days are long.

But this I know, that every Law
    That men have made for Man,
Since first Man took his brother's life,
    And this sad world began,
But straws the wheat and saves the chaff
    With a most evil fan.

[101]

This too I know — and wise it were
　　If each could know the same —
That every prison that men build
　　Is built with bricks of shame,
And bound with bars lest Christ should see
　　How men their brothers maim.

Oscar Wilde

THE MENAGERIE

Night in a County Workhouse

Oh come, ye lords and ladies of the realm,
Come from your couches soft, your perfumed halls,
Come watch with me throughout the weary hours.
Here are there sounds to thrill your jaded nerves,
Such as the cave-men, your forefathers, heard,
Crouching in forests of primeval night;
Here tier on tier in steel-barred cages pent
The beasts ye breed and hunt throughout the world.
Hark to that snore — some beast that slumbers deep;
Hark to that roar — some beast that dreams of blood;
Hark to that moan — some beast that wakes and weeps;
And then in sudden stillness mark the sound —
Some beast that rasps his vermin-haunted hide!

Oh come, ye lords and ladies of the realm,
Come keep the watch with me; this show is yours.
Behold the source of all your joy and pride,
The beasts ye harness fast and set to draw
The chariots of your pageantry and pomp!
It is their blood ye shed to make your feasts,
It is their treadmill that moves all your world.
Come gather now, and think how it will be

When God shall send His flaming angel down
And break these bars — so hath He done of yore,
So doeth He to lords and ladies grand —
And loose these beasts to raven in your streets!

Upton Sinclair

THE CHALLENGE OF THE TILLERS

Ye say to us, 'tis we who feed the world;
Ye give us loud enjoining of our task;
Ye scruple not the boon of boons to ask —
Our toil's allegiance to a flag unfurled.
Hear then our cry, in righteous anger hurled
Upon the easeful ones who blink and bask
Within the halls of greed, who wear the mask
Of truth, yet are as waiting adders curled:
How shall we serve you if ye possess the land?
How long shall we be herded like the kine
With mete and bound and harsh dividing line?
Without the soil, what use the willing hand?
If then your words be aught but mouthings vain,
Restore our rightful heritage again!

Richard Warner Borst

CALIBAN IN THE COAL MINES

God, we don't like to complain —
  We know that the mine is no lark —
But — there's the pools from the rain;
  But — there's the cold and the dark.

God, You don't know what it is —
  You, in Your well-lighted sky,
Watching the meteors whizz;
  Warm, with the sun always by.

[103]

God, if You had but the moon
   Stuck in Your cap for a lamp,
Even You'd tire of it soon,
   Down in the dark and the damp.

Nothing but blackness above,
   And nothing that moves but the cars —
God, if You wish for our love,
   Fling us a handful of stars!

Louis Untermeyer

SOCIETY

I looked and saw a splendid pageantry
Of beautiful women and of lordly men
Taking their pleasure in a flowery plain,
Where poppies and the red anemone
And many another leaf of cramoisy,
Flickered about their feet and gave their stain
To heels of iron or satin, and the grain
Of silken garments floating far and free,
As in the dance they wove themselves or strayed
By twos together, or lightly smiled and bowed,
Or courtesied to each other, or else played
At games of mirth and pastime, unafraid
In their delight; and all so high and proud,
They seemed scarce of the earth whereon they trod.

I looked again and saw that flowery space
Stirring, as if alive, beneath the tread
That rested now upon an old man's head,
And now upon a baby's gasping face,
Or mother's bosom or the rounded grace
Of a girl's throat; and what seemed the red

Of flowers was blood, in gouts and gushes shed
From hearts that broke under that frolic pace.
And now and then from out the dreadful floor
An arm or brow was lifted from the rest,
As if to strike in madness, or implore
For mercy; and anon some suffering breast
Heaved from the mass and sank; and as before
The revelers above them thronged and pressed.

William Dean Howells

FIFTH AVENUE, 1915

The motor cars go up and down,
  The painted ladies sit and smile.
  Along the sidewalks, mile on mile,
Parade the dandies of the town.

The latest hat, the latest gown,
  The tedium of their souls beguile.
The motor cars go up and down,
  The painted ladies sit and smile.

In wild and icy waters drown
  A thousand for a rock-bound isle.
  Ten thousand in a black defile
Perish for justice or a crown.
The motor cars go up and down. . . .

Hermann Hagedorn

TO A RICH YOUNG MAN

You wear a silken undervest and hose
  And all your garments are immaculate.
  No care disturbs your leisurely estate
When you are cushioned softly for repose

In a fair chamber kept by her deft hand,
Which, you assume, God made to cleanse your room —
The hand of servitude, of mop and broom,
　Of consecration to a boy's demand!

You have no purpose but to find some way
To entertain an idle mind all day
　At golf or with the decorated few.
　And yet, you are a man, to outward view!
A man — while women labor everywhere,
And you do naught for life but blink and stare!

Mary Craig Sinclair

THE JERICHO ROAD

I know the road to Jericho,
　It's in a part of town
That's full of factories and filth.
　I've seen the folk go down,

Small folk with roses in their cheeks
　And star-light in their eyes,
And seen them fall among the thieves,
　And heard their helpless cries

When toiling took their roses red
　And robbed them of their stars
And left them pale and almost dead.
　The while, in motor-cars

The priests and levites speeding by
　Read of the latest crimes
In headlines spread in black or red
　Across the " Evening Times."

How hard for those in limousines
  To heal the hurt of man!
It was a slow-paced ass that bore
  The Good Samaritan.

                    Edwin McNeill Poteat, Jr.

A Ballad of London

Ah, London! London! our delight,
Great flower that opens but at night,
Great City of the midnight sun,
Whose day begins when day is done.

Lamp after lamp against the sky
Opens a sudden beaming eye,
Leaping alight on either hand,
The iron lilies of the Strand.

Like dragonflies, the hansoms hover,
With jeweled eyes, to catch the lover:
The streets are full of lights and loves,
Soft gowns, and flutter of soiled doves.

The human moths about the light
Dash and cling close in dazed delight,
And burn and laugh, the world and wife,
For this is London, this is life!

Upon thy petals butterflies,
But at thy root, some say, there lies
A world of weeping trodden things,
Poor worms that have not eyes or wings.

From out corruption of their woe
Springs this bright flower that charms us so:
Men die and rot deep out of sight
To keep this jungle-flower bright.

JUSTICE

Paris and London, World-Flowers twain
Wherewith the World-Tree blooms again,
Since Time hath gathered Babylon,
And withered Rome still withers on.

Sidon and Tyre were such as ye,
How bright they shone upon the tree!
But Time hath gathered, both are gone,
And no man sails to Babylon.

Richard Le Gallienne

GUARDIANS OF A HOLY TRUST

Guardians of a holy trust
Who, in your rotting tenements,
Housed the people, till the offence
Rose to the Heaven of the Just —
Guardians of an ancient trust
Who, lately from these little ones
Dashed the cup of water: now
Bind new laurels to your brow,
Fling to the earth these sacred stones,
Give the altar to the dust!
Here the poor and friendless come —
Desolate the templed home
Of the friendless and the poor,
That your laurels may be sure!
Here beside the frowning walls
Where no more the wood-bird calls,
Where once the little children played,
Whose paradise ye have betrayed,
Here let the temple low be laid,
Here bring the altar to the dust —
Guardians of a holy trust!

Richard Watson Gilder

JUSTICE

▲

From BAD SQUIRE

A laborer in Christian England,
Where they cant of a Savior's name,
And yet waste men's lives like vermin's
For a few more brace of game.

. . . . .

We quarreled like brutes, and who wonders?
What self-respect could we keep,
Worse housed than your hacks and your pointers,
Worse fed than your hogs and your sheep?

Charles Kingsley

THE NEW ROME

A thousand starve, a few are fed,
　Legions of robbers rack the poor,
The rich man steals the widow's bread,
　And Lazarus dies at Dives' door;
The Lawyer and the Priest adjust
The claims of Luxury and Lust
To seize the earth and hold the soil,
　To store the grain they never reap;
Under their heels the white slaves toil,
　While children wail and women weep! —
The gods are dead, but in their name
Humanity is sold to shame,
While (then as now!) the tinsel'd Priest
Sitteth with robbers at the feast,
Blesses the laden blood-stain'd board,
Weaves garlands round the butcher's sword,
And poureth freely (now as then)
The sacramental blood of Men!

Robert Buchanan

[109]

▲

The Collection

I passed the plate in church.

There was little silver, but the crisp bank-notes heaped themselves up high before me;

And ever as the pile grew, the plate became warmer and warmer until it burned my fingers, and a smell of scorching flesh rose from it, and I perceived that some of the notes were beginning to smolder and curl, half-browned, at the edges.

And then I saw through the smoke into the very substance of the money, and I beheld what it really was;

I saw the stolen earnings of the poor, the wide margins of wages pared down to starvation;

I saw the underpaid factory girl eking out her living on the street, and the overworked child, and the suicide of the discharged miner;

I saw poisonous gases from great manufactories spreading disease and death;

I saw hideousness extending itself from coal mine and foundry over forest and river and field;

I saw money grabbed from fellow grabbers and swindlers, and underneath them the workman forever spinning it out of his vitals. . . .

I saw all this, and the plate burned my fingers so that I had to hold it first in one hand and then in the other; and I was glad when the parson in his white robes took the smoking pile from me on the chancel steps and, turning about, lifted it up and laid it on the altar.

It was an old-time altar indeed, for it bore a burnt offering of flesh and blood — a sweet savor unto the

Moloch whom these people worship with their daily
round of human sacrifices.
The shambles are in the temple as of yore, and the tables
of the money-changers, waiting to be overturned.

Ernest Howard Crosby

The Image in the Forum

Not Baal, but Christus-Jingo!   Heir
   Of Him who once was crucified!
The red stigmata still are there,
   The crimson spear-wounds in the side;
But raised aloft as God and Lord,
He holds the Money-bag and Sword.

See, underneath the Crown of Thorn,
   The eye-balls fierce, the features grim!
And merrily from night to morn
   We chant his praise and worship him
Great Christus-Jingo, at whose feet
Christian and Jew and Atheist meet!

A wondrous god! most fit for those
   Who cheat on 'Change, then creep to prayer;
Blood on his heavenly altar flows,
   Hell's burning incense fills the air,
And Death attests in street and lane
The hideous glory of his reign.

O gentle Jew, from age to age
   Walking the waves Thou could'st not tame,
This god hath ta'en Thy heritage,
   And stolen Thy sweet and stainless Name!
To him we crawl and bend the knee,
Naming Thy Name, but scorning Thee!

Robert Buchanan

In Bohemia

The thirsty of soul soon learn to know
The moistureless froth of the social show,
The vulgar sham of the pompous feast
Where the heaviest purse is the highest priest;
The organized charity, scrimped and iced,
In the name of a cautious, statistical Christ.

John Boyle O'Reilly

Holy Week

I cannot wax ecstatic with the throng
Of parasites and servitors, who pray
And make such vast ado, this week and day,
Over the details of an ancient wrong,
Yet in their soddenness themselves prolong
Still, for the son of man, Golgotha's way;
Who yet the slaving multitudes betray,
That they may share in Herod's dance and song.
I count remembrance of the martyred dead
Remembrance only worthy of esteem
When it bears onward still the martyr's dream,
And dares like protest for the common good.
They who stand well today with Caesar's brood
Call me in vain; so much they leave unsaid.

Robert Whitaker

In a Two Million Dollar Chapel

Brave bastion of a faith outworn,
  Designed by fear to baffle time . . .
As if the Cross were not enough
  To make a worship prayer sublime.

How hollow sounds the suppliant tread,
   How empty seems the crowded nave . . .
The chill of death without the worms;
   For worms would starve within this grave.

Too bright the lamps on gibbet chains,
   Too fine the gold that gleams above,
Too cold the walls, to make this place
   A house of worship and of love!

I cannot worship here, dear God, I cannot pray!
   I cannot find Thee here, so let me flee
Into the open air, somewhere away. . . .
   Where Love is, and where things are free!

                   Richard M. Steiner

PROFIT OR LOSS

In massive Gothic majesty it stands,
   Harbor of peace amid a sea of strife;
It offers to the sons of many lands
   A port and haven from the storm of life.

The cross of gold upon the spire's crest
   Gleamed like a beacon in the noonday sun;
The roofs and chimneys that beneath it pressed
   Seemed dwarfs and pigmies to the towers dun.

But now from windowed heights on every side,
   Turning the page of profit and of loss,
Far o'er the squirming, jostling human tide,
   Dollar-dimmed eyes look down upon the cross.

The market closes weak, the margin's small,
    Stocks are as vapor, bonds but bubbles; when
For loan of life there's no collateral,
    We must look upward to the cross again.

William B. Gilbert

No Resting Place

The Pastor says: " Happiness of the flesh
Nothing to do with the soul.
Only work; only endure;
Hardship and suffering are the Will of God.
Don't resist, but obey;
Wait till you die,
When the angel will receive you!
Amen! "

From the Church to the factory
Twelve hours' work,
Twelve hours' sweating,
Two small dimes for two " chins " of rice,
This is the blessing of the Lord;
Thank Him!
. . . In this glorious Shanghai!
Where many beautiful churches are seen,
But no resting place for the working men.

Tai Chi Tao
A leader of the Kuomingtang

Crusaders

They have taken the tomb of our Comrade Christ —
    Infidel hordes that believe not in Man;
Stable and stall for His birth sufficed,
    But His tomb is built on a kingly plan.

▲

They have hedged Him round with pomp and parade,
    They have buried Him deep under steel and stone —
But we come leading the great Crusade
    To give our Comrade back to His own.

Elizabeth Waddell

TO A PRINCE OF THE CHURCH

*Vestments valued at more than $1,000 were
menaced by the flames. . . . Cardinal —— was
recently presented with a jeweled chalice as a
testimony of love and esteem. . . . With the
coming of winter distress has become severe among
the strikers in the Pennsylvania-Ohio area. . . .*
                    (Miscellaneous press cuttings)
*"He that hath two coats, let him impart to him
    that hath none."* *(John the Baptist.)*

The vestments in your church, they say,
    Are rich with dyes and stiff with gold;
A thousand miners' kids today
    Hide in their shanties from the cold.

That chalice — gift of loving pride —
    The gems blaze as you lift it up;
A thousand babies, solemn-eyed,
    Click spoons within an empty cup.

So might I sling the sneering stone.
    But God will judge both me and you;
You sin not, nor are judged, alone.
    I had two coats; *I still have two.*

Kenneth W. Porter

[115]

Priest and Levite

They were a pattern to their age;
  No cause of charity they missed.
To keep their place upon the stage,
  They headed each subscription list;
" Would there were many more like them! "
Said all devout Jerusalem.

But when the desolate way they trod,
  And saw the traveler's pleading face,
When there was none to see but God,
  Their charity was out of place;
The case did not appeal to them
Outside their dear Jerusalem.

Edward Shillito

A Beggar in Paradise

My soul was beggar at the throne of God:
" Forgive it, Lord, if I have too soon sped
From the dear earth Thou gavest — for want of bread
My body died — under insensate clod
It lies, forgotten in the hearts of men,
And the cold snows have drifted and the wind
Between the stars rushes above it blind,
Against that day when clay shall rise again.

" ' Am I my brother's keeper? ' Thy people cry;
They wear self-righteousness like any cloak;
What matters it to them if beggars die! "
In wrath the Lord God out of heaven spoke:
" O men of earth, seed of the son of Cain,
My Son hath died for thee, and hath He died in vain? "

Verne Bright

ON SEEING A PICTURE OF CHRIST IN A JUNK SHOP

I walked today, along a city street
So squalid, so unclean, my whole soul shrank,
Revolted, from foul sights and odors rank.
Naught could I see in those I chanced to meet
Save hard or sodden faces, shambling feet,
Eyes bleared with vice and liquor. My soul drank
The lees of loathing. Then it was — I thank
Who willed it! — that a Face, austere and sweet
And strong and pure had stopped me, like a hand
Laid gently on me. O'er that thoroughfare
Of wretchedness and sin they looked, those eyes
Of One who was too tender to despise
The least, or of the lowest to despair.
Rebuked, I passed. The Christ must understand.

Marion W. Wildman

A WHITE WOMAN SPEAKS

*Lines written concerning an actual incident,
where a Negro, who had been acquitted by the
court, was taken by the mob and shot to death.*

So the law's agents left you to the throng;
You, whom the Court found innocent of wrong;
You, who could only stare and only sob;
They gave you over to that bawling mob,
Who shot at you like bullies from the back,
Because — poor devil — yes, your skin was black!

I do not pity you, my friend, who go
To sudden solitude of those who know
Only the ancient silences of death,
Who hear no more the feet of rain, the breath

Of low waves folding on the April seas,
But, Oh, deep in my heart I pity these
Poor human blunderers who have tonight
Made me, God knows, ashamed of being white!

Lucia Trent

BLACK MEN

Swift gusts of hollow night wind clatter by;
　　Tonight the earth is leper-pale and still.
The moon lies like a tombstone in the sky.
　　Three black men sway upon a lonely hill.

The pain has withered from each tortured face.
　　Soon earth will hide them with a mother's care;
But never God's great mercy can erase
　　A bitter scorn for men who hung them there.

Lucia Trent

From TO AMERICA

How would you have us, as we are?
Or sinking 'neath the load we bear,
Our eyes fixed forward on a star,
Or gazing empty at despair?

Rising or falling?　Men or things?
With dragging pace or footsteps fleet?
Strong, willing sinews in your wings,
Or tightening chains about your feet?

James Weldon Johnson
American Negro poet

I, Too

I, too, sing America.

I am the darker brother.
They send me in the kitchen
When company comes.
But I laugh,
And eat well,
And grow strong.

Tomorrow
I'll sit at the table
When company comes,
Nobody 'll dare
Say to me,
" Eat in the kitchen "
Then.

Besides, they'll see how beautiful I am
And be ashamed, —

I, too, am America.

Langston Hughes
American Negro poet

WE HAVE TOMORROW

We have tomorrow
Bright before us
Like a flame;

Yesterday, a night-gone thing
A sun-down name

And dawn today
Broad arch above the road we came,
We march.

Langston Hughes

From " The Crisis "

BATTLE HYMN OF THE CHINESE REVOLUTION
(1912)

Freedom, one of the greatest blessings of Heaven,
United to Peace, thou wilt work on this earth ten
thousand wonderful new things.

Grave as a spirit, great as a giant rising to the very skies,
With the clouds for a chariot and the wind for a steed,
Come, come to reign over the earth!

For the sake of the black hell of our slavery,
Come, enlighten us with a ray of thy sun! . . .

In this century we are working to open a new age.
In this century, with one voice, all virile men
Are calling for a new making of heaven and earth.

Hin-Yun, our ancestor, guide us!
Spirit of Freedom, come and protect us!

GÖTTERDÄMMERUNG

A god is dying, O bewildered ones,
A greybeard god whose zealous warriors
Have cowed the dismal world with bellowing guns
Until our sky like some vast conch-shell roars.
A god is perishing with glut of praise

From hypocrites whose tawney talons gleam
With secret gold which Judas-bright betrays
Sad barter of the birthright of their dream.

Let trumpets burn with turbulence of morn —
While Jericho cracks down its home of glass.
A god is dying and a man is born:
Let Mars and all his mangled mourners pass. . . .
Here raise the sepulcher of creeds and kings
Where peace, the Phoenix, lifts his golden wings!

Ernest Hartsock

From THE FOUR BROTHERS

Good-night is the word, good-night to the kings, to the
    czars,
      Good-night to the kaiser.
The breakdown and the fade-away begins.
The shadow of a great broom, ready to sweep out the
    trash, is here.

One finger is raised that counts the czar,
The ghost who beckoned men who come no more —
The czar gone to the winds on God's great dustpan,
The czar a pinch of nothing,
The last of the gibbering Romanoffs.

Out and good-night —
The ghosts of the summer palaces
And the ghosts of the winter palaces!
Out and out, good-night to the kings, the czars, the
    kaisers.

Another finger will speak,
And the kaiser, the ghost who gestures a hundred million
    sleeping-waking ghosts,

The kaiser will go onto God's great dustpan —
The last of the gibbering Hohenzollerns.

Look! God pities this trash, God waits with a broom
    and a dustpan,
God knows a finger will speak and count them out.

It is written in the stars;
It is spoken on the walls;
It clicks in the fire-white zigzag of the Atlantic wireless;
It mutters in the bastions of thousand-mile continents;
It sings in a whistle on the midnight winds from Walla
    Walla to Mesopotamia:
Out and good-night.

Carl Sandburg

How Long, O Lord!

Look down, O Lord, look down.   Are the centuries a
    waste?   Nigh upon two thousand years have gone
    since Thou didst walk the world, and the face of
    things is unchanged.
In Thy name now doth the Pharisee give alms in the
    street to the sound of a trumpet going before him.
In Thy name now doth the Levite pass by on the other
    side when a man hath fallen among thieves.
In Thy name now doth the lawyer lay on the poor bur-
    dens grievous to be borne.
In Thy name now doth the priest buy and sell the glad
    tidings of the kingdom, giving for the gospel of
    God the commandments of men, living in rich
    men's houses, faring sumptuously every day, pray-
    ing with his lips, " Give us this day our daily
    bread," but saying to his soul, " Soul, thou hast

much goods laid up for many years: take thine
ease, eat, drink, and be merry." Do men gather
grapes of thorns, or figs of thistles? Is it this Thy
gospel that yields that Thy fruit? Then will the
Master of the vineyard come shortly and say,
"Cut it down; why cumbereth it the ground?"

Hall Caine

THE MAN FORBID

This Beauty, this Divinity, this Thought,
This hallowed bower and harvest of delight
Whose roots ethereal seemed to clutch the stars,
Whose amaranths perfumed eternity,
Is fixed in earthly soil enriched with bones
Of used-up workers; fattened with the blood
Of prostitutes, the prime manure; and dressed
With brains of madmen and the broken hearts
Of children. Understand it, you at least
Who toil all day and writhe and groan all night
With roots of luxury, a cancer struck
In every muscle: out of you it is
Cathedrals rise and Heaven blossoms fair;
You are the hidden putrefying source
Of beauty and delight, of leisured hours,
Of passionate loves and high imaginings;
You are the dung that keeps the roses sweet.
I say, uproot it; plow the land; and let
A summer-fallow sweeten all the World.

John Davidson

NOBLEMEN

I fear the poor.
When I look in their faces, pinched and wan,
I shrink; my self-sufficiency is gone.
The consciousness sweeps through me, then:
These are the noblemen.

I fear the poor.
When I dole out to them as charity,
Some part of what belongs not unto me,
I marvel — cannot understand:
Why do they not demand?

I fear the poor.
I knew three brothers: two, that one might rise,
Were willing drudges; them dared he despise.
They bore it and forebore to show:
The highest are below.

Miles M. Dawson

BREAD AND ROSES

*In a parade of the strikers of Lawrence, Massachu-
setts, some young girls carried a banner inscribed,
" We want Bread, and Roses too! "*

As we come marching, marching, in the beauty of the
day,
A million darkened kitchens, a thousand mill-lofts gray
Are touched with all the radiance that a sudden sun dis-
closes,
For the people hear us singing, " Bread and Roses, Bread
and Roses."

JUSTICE

As we come marching, marching, we battle, too, for
    men —
For they are women's children and we mother them
    again.
Our lives shall not be sweated from birth until life
    closes —
Hearts starve as well as bodies: Give us Bread, but give
    us Roses!

As we come marching, marching, unnumbered women
    dead
Go crying through our singing their ancient song of
    Bread;
Small art and love and beauty their drudging spirits
    knew —
Yes, it is bread we fight for — but we fight for Roses,
    too.

As we come marching, marching, we bring the Greater
    Days —
The rising of the women means the rising of the race —
No more the drudge and idler — ten that toil where one
    reposes —
But a sharing of life's glories: Bread and Roses, Bread
    and Roses!

James Oppenheim

To the Free Children

We of our generation
who touched liberty
had to leap for it.
Not as over a chasm
aided by the momentum of running feet;

but up in air . . . one glimpse . . .
lash-breadth of glory
  white as flame on snow . . .
then shock of falling backward . . .
. . . you
we hold high above our heads.

II

We hear you knocking at our doors,
little white runners before the dawn.
We arise and accompany you forth . . .
but slowly . . .
for we
need our staffs.

III

Not as through smoked glasses
shall you look upon liberty,
but with the unflinching gaze
as the desert-born
looks in the face of the sun.

IV

Remember
when the dawn breaks
those who led you through the night . . .
as the blind guided through the darkness
at Pompeii
those who had eyes.

Lola Ridge

A Fence

Now the stone house on the lake front is finished and
the workmen are beginning the fence.
The palings are made of iron bars with steel points that
can stab the life out of any man who falls on them.
As a fence, it is a masterpiece, and will shut off the rabble
and all vagabonds and hungry men and all wandering children looking for a place to play.
Passing through the bars and over the steel points will
go nothing except Death and the Rain and Tomorrow.

Carl Sandburg

From a New York Skyscraper

O sprawling city! worlds in a world!
What means the Ghetto to Morningside?

.   .   .   .   .

Why, the souls in one car where they hang on the straps,
Could send this city a-wing from the sod.
Each man is a tiny faucet that taps the infinite reservoir
of God!
What if they turned the faucet full-stream?
What if our millions tonight were aware?
What if tomorrow they built in their dream the City of
Brothers in laughter and prayer?

James Oppenheim

CRY OF THE PEOPLE

Tremble before your chattels,
   Lords of the scheme of things!
Fighters of all earth's battles,
   Ours is the might of kings!
Guided by seers and sages,
   The world's heart-beat for a drum,
Snapping the chains of ages,
   Out of the night we come!

Lend us no ear that pities!
   Offer no almoner's hand!
Alms for the builders of cities!
   When will you understand?
Down with your pride of birth
   And your golden gods of trade!
A man is worth to his mother, Earth,
   All that a man has made!

We are the workers and makers!
   We are no longer dumb!
Tremble, O Shirkers and Takers!
   Sweeping the earth — we come!
Ranked in the world-wide dawn,
   Marching into the day!
The night is gone and the sword is drawn
   And the scabbard is thrown away!

                       John G. Neihardt

WE WHOM THE DEAD HAVE NOT FORGIVEN

I cry to the mountains; I cry to the sea —
I cry to the forest to cover me
From the terror of the invisible throng

▲

With marching feet the whole day long —
The whole night long.
Beating the accent of their wrong.

We whom the Dead have not forgiven
Must hear forever that ominous beat,
For the free, light, rippled air of heaven
Is burdened now with dead men's feet:

Feet that make solid the fluid space,
Feet that make weary the tireless wind,
Feet that leave grime on the moon's white face —
Black is the moon for us who have sinned!

And the mountains will not cover us,
Nor yet the forest nor the sea;
No storm of human restlessness
Can wake the tide or bend the tree.

Forever and ever until we die,
Through the once sweet air and the once blue sky
The thud of feet — the invisible throng,
Beating the accent of their wrong.

Sara Bard Field

INJUSTICE

Be still, my soul, be still; the arms you bear are brittle,
   Earth and high heaven are fixt of old and founded
      strong.
Think rather — call to thought, if now you grieve a
   little,
   The days when we had rest, O soul, for they were long.

Men loved unkindness then, but lightless in the quarry
   I slept and saw not; tears fell down, I did not mourn;

Sweat ran and blood sprang out and I was never sorry:
    Then it was well with me, in days ere I was born.

Now, and I muse for why and never find the reason,
    I pace the earth, and drink the air, and feel the sun.
Be still, be still, my soul; it is but for a season:
    Let us endure an hour and see injustice done.

Ay, look: high heaven and earth ail from the prime
        foundation;
    All thoughts to rive the heart are here, and all are
        vain:
Horror and scorn and hate and fear and indignation —
    Oh, why did I awake? when shall I sleep again?

A. E. Housman

From " A Shropshire Lad "

THE VOICE UNTO PHARAOH

*" And the children . . . sighed by reason of their
bondage, and they cried, and their cry came up
unto God." — Exodus 2:23.*

Pharaoh, Pharaoh, let my people go!

My fettered children toil with aching limbs
    And wearied fingers, brain and spirit bound.
Their puny forms are bent; the shadow dims
    Their straining eyes; their ears are choked with
        sound
And thick with reek is every breath they draw.
    I gave them light to see and song to hear;
I gave them Truth for guide and Love for law;
    And *thou* hast given darkness, blight and fear.

[130]

Pharaoh, Pharaoh, let my people go!

In chains, unseen but strong, my children slave,
Too dull for hopes or dreams, too dumb for prayers;
Thou, thou hast robbed them of the youth I gave,
The world I made, the joy that should be theirs;
These lives are coined to swell thy glittering store;
Then darest thou plead, " Nay, Lord, I did not
know! " —
Still heaping up their burdens more and more?
The sand is running. Let my people go.

Pharaoh, Pharaoh, let my people go!

Thy heart is hard. Be warned: The Plagues shall
come.
This wrong thou dost shall breed yet fouler wrong.
Those lips shall speak in flame that now are dumb;
Those feeble hands, through wrath and hatred
strong,
Shall rend where they have wrought. Yea, once again
Disease, Rebellion, Crime shall overthrow
The selfishness that bred them. Sons of men,
For dread of vengeance, let my people go!
Arthur Guiterman

POEMS OF
JUSTICE

▲▲▲▲▲▲▲▲▲▲▲▲

BROTHERS
ALL

▼

A Consecration

Not of the princes and prelates with periwigged
    charioteers
Riding triumphantly laureled to lap the fat of the years,
Rather the scorned — the rejected — the men hemmed
    in with the spears;

The men of the tattered battalion which fights till it
    dies,
Dazed with the dust of the battle, the din and the cries,
The men with the broken heads and the blood running
    into their eyes.

Not the be-medaled Commander, beloved of the throne,
Riding cock-horse to parade when the bugles are blown,
But the lads who carried the koppie and cannot be
    known.

Not the ruler for me, but the ranker, the tramp of the
    road,
The slave with the sack on his shoulders pricked on with
    the goad,
The man with too weighty a burden, too weary a load.

The sailor, the stoker of steamers, the man with the clout,
The chantyman bent at the halliards putting a tune to
    the shout,
The drowsy man at the wheel and the tired lookout.

Others may sing of the wine and the wealth and the
    mirth,

▲

The portly presence of potentates goodly in girth; —
Mine be the dirt and the dross, the dust and scum of the
earth!

Theirs be the music, the color, the glory, the gold;
Mine be a handful of ashes, a mouthful of mold.
Of the maimed, of the halt and the blind in the rain
and the cold —

Of these shall my songs be fashioned, my tale be told.

John Masefield

THE TEARS OF THE OPPRESSED

Then I returned and saw all oppressions that are done
under the sun: and behold, the tears of such as were
oppressed, and they had no comforter; and on the
side of their oppressors there was power, but they
had no comforter.

The Book of Ecclesiastes

" GOOD TIDINGS UNTO THE MEEK "

The Lord hath anointed me to preach good tidings unto
the meek; he hath sent me to bind up the broken-
hearted, to proclaim liberty to the captives.
They shall build the old wastes, they shall raise up the
former desolations, and they shall repair the waste
cities.

Isaiah
Hebrew prophet, 8th century, B.C.

PROSPERITY

Thou hast taken pledges of thy brother for naught, and
stripped the naked of their clothing. Thou hast
not given water to the weary to drink, and thou
hast withholden bread from the hungry.

But as for the mighty man, he had the earth; and the
honorable man, he dwelt in it.

Thou hast sent widows away empty, and the arms of
the fatherless have been broken.

The Book of Job

CONCERNING USURY

To him who is of kin to thee give his due, and to the
poor and to the wayfarer: this will be best for those
who seek the face of God; and with them it shall
be well.

Whatever ye put out at usury to increase it with the
substance of others shall have no increase from God:
but whatever ye shall give in alms, as seeking the
face of God, shall be doubled to you.

The Koran

THE GROANS OF WOUNDED SOULS

Take heed that he weep not; for the throne of the
Almighty is shaken to and fro when the orphan sets
a-crying.

Beware of the groans of the wounded souls, since the
hidden sore will at length break out; oppress not
to the utmost a single heart, for a single sigh has
power to overset a whole world.

Sadi
Persian Poet, A.D. 1200

▲

BROTHERHOOD

Your task is to form the universal family, to build the
City of God, and by a continuous labor gradually
to translate his work in humanity into fact.
When you love one another as brothers, and treat each
other reciprocally as such; when each one, seeking
his own good in the good of all, shall identify his
own life with the life of all, his own interests with
the interests of all, and shall be always ready to
sacrifice himself for all the members of the common
family — then most of the ills which weigh upon
the human race will vanish, as thick mists gathered
upon the horizon vanish at the rising of the sun.

Robert de Lamennais

From " The Book of the People "

"WHEN I THINK OF THE HUNGRY PEOPLE"

I have a suit of new clothes in this happy new year;
    Hot rice cake soup is excellent to my taste;
But when I think of the hungry people in this city,
    I am ashamed of my fortune in the presence of God.

O-Shi-O
Japanese scholar, 18th century

FOR A' THAT AND A' THAT

Is there for honest poverty
That hangs his head, and a' that?
The coward slave, we pass him by;
We dare be poor for a' that!

[138]

JUSTICE

For a' that, and a' that,
Our toils obscure, and a' that;
The rank is but the guinea stamp —
The man's the gowd for a' that!

What tho' on hamely fare we dine,
Wear hodden gray, and a' that?
Gie fools their silks, and knaves their wine —
A man's a man for a' that!
For a' that, and a' that,
Their tinsel show, and a' that;
The honest man, though e'er sae poor,
Is king o' men, for a' that!

Ye see yon birkie ca'd a lord,
Wha struts, an' stares, an' a' that —
Tho' hundreds worship at his word,
He's but a coof for a' that;
For a' that, and a' that,
His riband, star, and a' that;
The man of independent mind,
He looks an' laughs at a' that.

A prince can mak a belted knight,
A marquis, duke, and a' that;
But an honest man's aboon his might —
Gude faith, he mauna fa' that!
For a' that, and a' that,
Their dignities, and a' that;
The pith o' sense, and pride o' worth,
Are higher rank than a' that.

Then let us pray that come it may —
As come it will for a' that —
That sense and worth, o'er a' the earth,
May bear the gree, and a' that.

For a' that, and a' that,
It's comin' yet, for a' that —
That man to man, the warld o'er,
Shall brithers be for a' that.

Robert Burns

From LOCKSLEY HALL FIFTY YEARS AFTER

Is it well that while we range with Science, glorying in
the time,
City children soak and blacken soul and sense in city
slime?
There among the gloomy alleys Progress halts on palsied
feet;
Crime and hunger cast out maidens by the thousand on
the street;

There the master scrimps his haggard seamstress of her
daily bread;
There the single sordid attic holds the living and the
dead;
There the smoldering fire of fever creeps across the
rotted floor,
And the crowded couch of incest, in the warrens of the
poor.

Alfred Tennyson

From THE DESERTED VILLAGE

Ill fares the land, to hastening ills a prey,
Where wealth accumulates, and men decay:
Princes and lords may flourish, or may fade —
A breath can make them, as a breath has made:

JUSTICE

But a bold peasantry, their country's pride,
When once destroyed, can never be supplied.
A time there was, ere England's griefs began,
When every rood of ground maintained its man;
For him light labor spread her wholesome store,
Just gave what life required, but gave no more:
His best companions, innocence and health;
And his best riches, ignorance of wealth.

But times are altered: trade's unfeeling train
Usurp the land, and dispossess the swain;
Along the lawn, where scattered hamlets rose,
Unwieldy wealth and cumbrous pomp repose;
And every want to luxury allied,
And every pang that folly pays to pride,
Those gentle hours that plenty bade to bloom,
Those calm desires that asked but little room,
Those healthful sports that graced the peaceful scene,
Lived in each look, and brightened all the green —
These, far departing, seek a kinder shore,
And rural mirth and manners are no more. . . .

Ye friends to truth, ye statesmen, who survey
The rich man's joys increase, the poor's decay,
'Tis yours to judge how wide the limits stand
Between a splendid and a happy land.

. . . . .

Oliver Goldsmith

BALLADE OF MISERY AND IRON

Several years ago the Century Magazine received several poems from an inmate of the State penitentiary of Minnesota. Upon investigation it was found that the poet, George Carter, a young Englishman, had been driven to stealing by starvation. Subsequently his pardon was procured.

Haggard faces and trembling knees,
   Eyes that shine with a weakling's hate,
Lips that mutter their blasphemies,
   Murderous hearts that darkly wait:
   These are they who were men of late,
Fit to hold a plow or a sword.
   If a prayer this wall may penetrate,
Have pity on these my comrades, Lord!

Poets sing of life at the lees
   In tender verses and delicate;
Of tears and manifold agonies —
   Little they know of what they prate.
   Out of this silence, passionate
Sounds a deeper, a wilder chord.
   If sound be heard through the narrow grate,
Have pity on these my comrades, Lord!

Hark, that wail of the distant breeze,
   Piercing ever the close-barred gate,
Fraught with torturing memories
   Of eyes that kindle and lips that mate.
   Ah, by the loved ones desolate,
Whose anguish never can pen record,
   If Thou be truly compassionate,
Have pity on these my comrades, Lord!

JUSTICE

▲

L'ENVOI

These are pawns that the hand of Fate
    Careless sweeps from the checker-board.
Thou that know'st if the game be straight,
    Have pity on these my comrades, Lord!

George Carter

COUNTRY LIFE

Or will you deem them amply paid in health,
Labor's fair child, that languishes with wealth?
Go then! and see them rising with the sun,
Through a long course of daily toil to run;
See them beneath the dog-star's raging heat,
When the knees tremble and the temples beat;
Behold them, leaning on their scythes, look o'er
The labor past, and toils to come explore;
See them alternate suns and showers engage,
And hoard up aches and anguish for their age;
Through fens and marshy moors their steps pursue,
Where their warm pores imbibe the evening dew;
Then own that labor may as fatal be
To these thy slaves, as thine excess to thee.

George Crabbe
" Poet of the Poor "

From THE LOST JOY

We toil in the dark coal mines underground,
Where death waits in the blackness —
Our labor has no joy.
We toil in the great steel mills,
Where our souls are burnt,

Our bodies bartered for a crust.
If you had toiled as we have toiled,
You would not sing of joy.
We are the children from the factories' gloom.
We know what labor is,
For it has stooped our bodies,
Crushed our souls —
But what is this thing you call joy?

. . . . . .

Whence comes this strange and shuddering sound
That wails throughout the blackness?
It is the voice of Labor
Crying for the lost joy!

Ruth Le Prade

Two Men I Honor

Two men I honor and no third. First, the toilworn
craftsman that with earth-made implements labori-
ously conquers the earth and makes her man's.

Venerable to me is the hard hand.

Venerable too is the rugged face. Oh, but the more
venerable for thy rudeness, and even because we
must pity as well as love thee!

Hardly entreated brother! For us was thy back so bent.

It is not because of his toils that I lament for the poor.
The poor is hungry and athirst, but for him also
there is food and drink.

He is heavy laden and weary; but for him also the
heavens send sleep.

[144]

▲

What I *do* mourn over is that the lamp of his soul should
go out. Alas, while the body stands so broad and
brawny, must the soul lie blinded, dwarfed, stupe-
fied, almost annihilated!

That there should one man die ignorant who had capacity
for knowledge, this I call a tragedy.

A second man I honor, and still more highly: him who
is seen toiling for the spiritually indispensable; not
daily bread but the Bread of Life.

Is not he too in his duty?

(He is) not earthly craftsman only, but inspired thinker,
who with heaven-made implement conquers heaven
for us.

These two, in all their degrees, I honor; all else is chaff
and dust.

Thomas Carlyle

A Parable

Said Christ our Lord, " I will go and see
How the men, my brethren, believe in me."
He passed not again through the gate of birth,
But made himself known to the children of earth.

Then said the chief priests, and rulers, and kings,
" Behold, now, the Giver of all good things;
Go to, let us welcome with pomp and state
Him who alone is mighty and great."

With carpets of gold the ground they spread
Wherever the Son of Man should tread,

And in palace-chambers lofty and rare
They lodged Him, and served Him with kingly fare.

Great organs surged through arches dim
Their jubilant floods in praise of Him;
And in church, and palace, and judgment-hall,
He saw His own image high over all.

But still, wherever His steps they led,
The Lord in sorrow bent down His head,
And from under the heavy foundation-stones,
The son of Mary heard bitter groans.

And in church, and palace, and judgment-hall,
He marked great fissures that rent the wall,
And opened wider and yet more wide
As the living foundation heaved and sighed.

" Have ye founded your thrones and altars, then,
On the bodies and souls of living men?
And think ye that building shall endure,
Which shelters the noble and crushes the poor?

" With gates of silver and bars of gold
Ye have fenced my sheep from their Father's fold;
I have heard the dropping of their tears
In heaven these eighteen hundred years."

" O Lord and Master, not ours the guilt,
We build but as our fathers built;
Behold Thine images, how they stand,
Sovereign and sole, through all our land.

" Our task is hard — with sword and flame
To hold Thine earth forever the same,
And with sharp crooks of steel to keep
Still, as Thou leftest them, Thy sheep."

▲

Then Christ sought out an artisan,
A low-browed, stunted, haggard man,
And a motherless girl, whose fingers thin
Pushed from her faintly want and sin.

These set He in the midst of them,
And as they drew back their garment-hem,
For fear of defilement, " Lo, here," said He,
" The images ye have made of me! "

James Russell Lowell

BEFORE

Before I brand a brother
    With envy or with shame,
I'll whisper to my heart, " He comes
    The road I came."

If any sue for pity —
    Though friend he be or foe —
I'll whisper to my soul, " He goes
    The road I go."

Mary Sinton Leitch

MY RELIGION

What is the law of nature? Is it to know that my
    security and that of my family, all my amusements
    and pleasures, are purchased at the expense of
    misery, deprivation, and suffering to thousands of
    human beings — by the terror of the gallows; by
    the misfortune of thousands stifling within prison
    walls; by the fears inspired by millions of soldiers
    and guardians of civilization, torn from their
    homes and besotted by discipline, to protect our

pleasures with loaded revolvers against the possible interference of the famishing?

Is it to purchase every fragment of bread that I put in my mouth and the mouths of my children by the numberless privations that are necessary to procure my abundance?

Or is it to be certain that my piece of bread only belongs to me when I know that everyone else has a share, and that no one starves while I eat?

Leo Tolstoy

THE POOR

Among the mountains I wandered and saw blue haze and red crag and was amazed;

On the beach where the long push under the endless tide maneuvers, I stood silent;

Under the stars on the prairie watching the Dipper slant over the horizon's grass, I was full of thoughts.

Great men, pageants of war and labor, soldiers and workers, mothers lifting their children — these all I touched, and felt the solemn thrill of them.

And then one day I got a true look at the Poor, millions of the Poor, patient and toiling; more patient than crags, tides, and stars; innumerable, patient as the darkness of night — and all broken, humble ruins of nations.

Carl Sandburg

ON A STEAMSHIP

All night, without the gates of slumber lying,
I listen to the joy of falling water,
And to the throbbing of an iron heart.

In ages past, men went upon the sea,
Waiting the pleasure of the chainless winds;
But now the course is laid, the billows part;
Mankind has spoken: " Let the ship go there! "

I am grown haggard and forlorn, from dreams
That haunt me, of the time that is to be,
When man shall cease from wantonness and strife,
And lay his law upon the course of things.
Then shall he live no more on sufferance,
An accident, the prey of powers blind;
The untamed giants of nature shall bow down —
The tides, the tempest and the lightning cease
From mockery and destruction, and be turned
Unto the making of the soul of man.

Upton Sinclair

From GLOUCESTER MOORS

God, dear God!   Does she know her port,
    Though she goes so far about?
Or blind astray, does she make her sport
    To brazen and chance it out?
I watched when her captains passed:
    She were better captainless.
Men in the cabin, before the mast,
But some were reckless and some aghast,
    And some sat gorged at mess.

By her battened hatch I leaned and caught
    Sounds from the noisome hold —
Cursing and sighing of souls distraught
    And cries too sad to be told.
Then I strove to go down and see;
    But they said, " Thou art not of us! "

I turned to those on the deck with me
And cried, " Give help! " · But they said, " Let be:
   Our ship sails faster thus."

Jill-o'er-the-ground is purple blue,
   Blue is the quaker-maid,
The alder-clump where the brook comes through
   Breeds cresses in its shade.
To be out of the moiling street,
   With its swelter and its sin!
Who has given to me this sweet,
And given my brother dust to eat?
   And when will his wage come in?

Scattering wide or blown in ranks,
   Yellow and white and brown,
Boats and boats from the fishing banks
   Come home to Gloucester town.
There is cash to purse and spend,
   There are wives to be embraced,
Hearts to borrow and hearts to lend,
And hearts to take and keep to the end —
   O little sails, make haste!

But thou, vast outbound ship of souls,
   What harbor town for thee?
What shapes, when thy arriving tolls,
   Shall crowd the banks to see?
Shall all the happy shipmates then
   Stand singing brotherly?
Or shall a haggard ruthless few
   Warp her over and bring her to,
While the many broken souls of men
Fester down in the slaver's pen,
   And nothing to say or do?

William Vaughn Moody

FREEDOM

Men! whose boast it is that ye
Come of fathers brave and free,
If there breathe on earth a slave,
Are ye truly free and brave?
If ye do not feel the chain
When it works a brother's pain,
Are ye not base slaves indeed,
Slaves unworthy to be freed?

Is true Freedom but to break
Fetters for our own dear sake,
And, with leathern hearts, forget
That we owe mankind a debt?
No!   True Freedom is to share
All the chains our brothers wear,
And, with heart and hand, to be
Earnest to make others free!

They are slaves who fear to speak
For the fallen and the weak;
They are slaves who will not choose
Hatred, scoffing and abuse,
Rather than in silence shrink
From the truth they needs must think:
They are slaves who dare not be
In the right with two or three.

James Russell Lowell

Let Man Serve Law for Man

Let man serve law for man;
Live for friendship, live for love,
For truth's and harmony's behoof;
The state may follow how it can,
As Olympus follows Jove.

Ralph Waldo Emerson

To a Republican Friend

God knows it, I am with you. If to prize
Those virtues, prized and practised by too few,
But prized, but loved, but eminent in you,
Man's fundamental life; if to despise

The barren optimistic sophistries
Of comfortable moles, whom what they do
Teaches the limit of the just and true
(And for such doing they require not eyes);

If sadness at the long heart-wasting show
Wherein earth's great ones are disquieted;
If thoughts, not idle, while before me flow

The armies of the homeless and unfed —
If these are yours, if this is what you are,
Then am I yours, and what you feel, I share.

Yet, when I muse on what life is, I seem
Rather to patience prompted, than that proud
Prospect of hope which France proclaims so loud —

.   .   .   .   .

[152]

▲

Nor will that day dawn at a human nod,
When, bursting through the network superposed
By selfish occupation — plot and plan,

Lust, avarice, envy — liberated man,
All difference with his fellow-mortal closed,
Shall be left standing face to face with God.

Matthew Arnold

From The Vision of Sir Launfal

And the voice that was softer than silence said,
" Lo, it is I, be not afraid!
In many climes, without avail,
Thou hast spent thy life for the Holy Grail;
Behold, it is here — this cup which thou
Didst fill at the streamlet for me but now;
This crust is my body broken for thee,
This water his blood that died on the tree;
The Holy Supper is kept, indeed,
In whatso we share with another's need;
Not what we give, but what we share,
For the gift without the giver is bare;
Who gives himself with his alms feeds three,
Himself, his hungering neighbor, and me."

James Russell Lowell

" Scum o' the Earth "

I

At the gate of the West I stand,
On the isle where the nations throng.
We call them " scum o' the earth ";

Stay, are we doing you wrong,
Young fellow from Socrates' land? —

JUSTICE

You, like a Hermes so lissome and strong
Fresh from the Master Praxiteles' hand?
So you're of Spartan birth?
Descended, perhaps from one of the band —
Deathless in story and song —
Who combed their long hair at Thermopylæ's pass?
Ah, I forget what straits, alas!
More tragic than theirs, more compassion-worth,
Have doomed you to march in our " immigrant class "
When you're nothing but " scum o' the earth."

II

You Pole with the child on your knee,
What dower bring you to the land of the free?
Hark! does she croon
That sad little tune
That Chopin once found on his Polish lea
And mounted in gold for you and for me?
Now a ragged young fiddler answers
In wild Czech melody
That Dvorak took whole from the dancers.
And the heavy faces bloom
In the wonderful Slavic way;
The little dull eyes, the brows agloom,
Suddenly dawn like the day.
While, watching these folk and their mystery,
I forget that we,
In our scornful mirth,
Brand them as " polaks " — and " scum o' the earth."

III

Genoese boy of the level brow,
Lad of the lustrous dreamy eyes

[154]

JUSTICE

Astare at Manhattan's pinnacles now
In the first sweet shock of a hushed surprise;
Within your far-rapt seer's eyes
I catch the glow of the wild surmise
That played on the Santa Maria's prow
In that still gray dawn,
Four centuries gone,
When a world from the wave began to rise.
Oh, who shall foretell what high emprise
Is the goal that gleams
When Italy's dreams
Spread wing and sweep into the skies.
Cæsar dreamed him a world ruled well;
Dante dreamed Heaven out of Hell;
Angelo brought us there to dwell;
And you, are you of a different birth? —
You're only a " dago " — and " scum o' the earth "!

IV

Stay, are we doing you wrong
Calling you " scum o' the earth,"
Man of the sorrow-bowed head,
Of the features tender yet strong —
Man of the eyes full of wisdom and mystery
Mingled with patience and dread?
Have not I known you in history,
Sorrow-bowed head?
Were you the poet-king, worth
Treasures of Ophir unpriced?
Were you the prophet, perchance, whose art
Foretold how the rabble would mock
That shepherd of spirits, erelong,
Who should carry the lambs on his heart
And tenderly feed his flock?

[155]

▲

Man — lift that sorrow-bowed head.
Behold the face of the Christ!

The vision dies at its birth.
You're merely a butt for a mirth.
You're a " sheeny " — and therefore despised
And rejected as " scum o' the earth."

v

Countrymen, bend and invoke
Mercy for us blasphemers,
For that we spat on these marvelous folk,
Nations of darers and dreamers,
Scions of singers and seers,
Our peers, and more than our peers.
" Rabble and refuse," we name them
And " scum o' the earth " to shame them.
Mercy for us of the few, young years,
Of the culture so callow and crude,
Of the hands so grasping and rude,
The lips so ready for sneers
At the sons of our ancient more-than-peers.
Mercy for us who dare despise
Men in whose loins our Homer lies;
Mothers of men who shall bring to us
The glory of Titian, the grandeur of Huss;
Children in whose frail arms shall rest
Prophets and singers and saints of the West.
Newcomers all from the eastern seas,
Help us incarnate dreams like these.
Forget and forgive that we did you wrong.
Help us to father a nation, strong
In the comradeship of an equal birth,
In the wealth of the richest bloods of earth.

Robert Haven Schauffler

Under the Tan

Italians, Magyars, aliens all —
  Human under the tan —
Eyes that can smile when their fellows call,
  A spike-driver each, but a man.
Rumble and roar! On the tracks they lay
  We ride in our parlor car.
Spades on their shoulders, they give us way,
  Lords of the near and the far.

Polack and Slav and dark-eyed Greek —
  Human under the tan —
Up go their hands, and their faces speak,
  Saluting us, man and man.
Cushioned seats, and our souls at ease,
  Dainty in food and fare,
We are the masters their toil must please,
  Or face gaunt-cheeked despair.

Russian and Irishman, Croat and Swede —
  Human under the tan —
Giving us homage while making us speed,
  As only the generous can,
Riding and riding, hats in our hands,
  Something warm in the eye,
Fellows, in spite of your skins and lands,
  We greet you rushing by.

Lewis Worthington Smith

The Immigrant Madonna

This Christmastide, America, I bring to you my son,
My baby son.
He comes with little heritage,

But his eyes are clear, his body strong.
He is ready for you to do with him what you will.
What will you?

Will you use him hurriedly for your quick ends?
And will you then discard him because he is worn out —
  and still a foreigner?
Or will you teach him, watch him grow and help him
  to be one of you,
To work with you for those great things you seek?

He is my son, America,
And all my treasure.
I bring him here to you —
And you, what will you do with him?

       Helen Dwight Fisher

PROVINCIALISM

I judge all the Dagoes by Tony Cattini,
I judge all the Japs by the one that I know,
I judge all the Slovaks by Moritz Koppini,
I judge all the Chinks by my wash-man, Wing Po.

I judge all the Spaniards by Pedro Garcia,
I judge all the French by Alphonse de Bernard,
I judge the Egyptians by Ibin Ben Kia,
I judge all the Hindus by Boma Singh Kard.

I ain't traveled far from the place I was born in,
But I've seen the world, for it's all come to me;
Some odd foreign face I meet up with each mornin'
From countries way off, beyond the deep sea.

You can't tell me much about these strange races,
For ain't I seen all of 'em, right in this town.

▲

I know their queer dress, and their funny shaped faces —
White, black, red and yeller, and lots of 'em brown.

They're diff'rent from us, and I'm blamed if I like 'em,
They talk in a lingo you can't understand;
They make me so mad that I most want to strike 'em,
Why didn't they stay in their own foreign land?

Of course, they may have me in close observation,
To find out what kind of a man I may be;
But how can they know of our glorious nation?
I wonder if they judge *my* country by *me*?

Aubert Edgar Bruce

TRASH

Three weeks I trekked the woods without a trail
   And found no sign of man upon the earth;
My zest in solitude began to fail;
   I longed for human speech and song and mirth,
Until I chanced on rubbish in a pile,
   And beamed at broken saws, charred rabbit skin,
Hobnails, a nine of hearts, a flask, a file,
   And sweet lips on a crushed tobacco tin.
If I were driven from earth by a flaming lash,
   To roam the flinty rocks of Capricorn,
I think no sorriest bit of human trash
   Would be abject enough to win my scorn;
      I'd find the sodden hobo sage and clean,
      Own brother to the vagrant Nazarene.

Robert Haven Schauffler

JUSTICE

▲

From WORK GANGS

People singing; people with song mouths connecting
    with song hearts; people who must sing or die;
    people whose song hearts break if there is no song
    mouth; these are my people.

Carl Sandburg

THE BREAD LINE

Well, here they are — they stand and stamp and shiver
    Waiting their food from some kind stranger hand,
Their weary limbs with eagerness a-quiver
    Hungry and heartsick in a bounteous land.

"Beggars and bums?" Perhaps, and largely worthless.
    Shaky with drink, unlovely, craven, low,
With obscene tongues and hollow laughter mirthless;
    But who shall give them scorn for being so?

Yes, here they are — with gaunt and pallid faces,
    With limbs ill-clad and fingers stiff and blued,
Shuffling and stamping on their pavement places,
    Waiting and watching for their bit of food.

We boast of vast achievements and of power,
    Of human progress knowing no defeat,
Of strange new marvels every day and hour —
    And here's the bread line in the wintry street!

Ten thousand years of war and peace and glory,
    Of hope and work and deeds and golden schemes,
Of mighty voices raised in song and story,
    Of huge inventions and of splendid dreams;

JUSTICE

▲

Ten thousand years replete with every wonder,
  Of empires risen and of empires dead;
Yet still, while wasters roll in swollen plunder,
  These broken men must stand in line — for bread!

Berton Braley

The Factories

I have shut my little sister in from life and light
  (For a rose, for a ribbon, for a wreath across my hair),
I have made her restless feet still until the night,
  Locked from sweets of summer and from wild spring
    air;
I who ranged the meadow lands, free from sun to sun,
  Free to sing and pull the buds and watch the far wings
    fly,
I have bound my sister till her playing-time is done —
  Oh, my little sister, was it I? — was it I?

I have robbed my sister of her day of maidenhood
  (For a robe, for a feather, for a trinket's restless
    spark),
Shut from Love till dusk shall fall, how shall she know
    good,
  How shall she pass scatheless through the sinlit dark?
I who could be innocent, I who could be gay,
  I who could have love and mirth before the light
    went by,
I have put my sister in her mating-time away —
  Sister, my young sister, — was it I? — was it I?

I have robbed my sister of the lips against her breast
  (For a coin, for the weaving of my children's lace and
    lawn),

[161]

Feet that pace beside the loom, hands that cannot rest,
  How can she know motherhood, whose strength is
      gone?
I who took no heed of her, starved and labor-worn,
  I against whose placid heart my sleepy gold heads lie,
Round my path they cry to me, little souls unborn,
  God of Life — Creator! It was I! It was I!

                              Margaret Widdemer

Sweat-Shop Slaves

I see my white-faced sisters of the foul tenements
Stooping over their needles,
Which flash faster than the wings of the dragon-fly,
Or the fangs of the quick-coiling serpent.
Their fingers are yellow, the fingers of the dead;
The thin fingers of those who have died of hunger.
Without pause, not daring to lose a moment,
They snatch at the crust of their starvation;
Bending close above the garments,
And the murmur of their hearts is continually:
" Lest we starve! Lest we starve! "

I see my haggard sisters of the prisoning factories;
Their eyes sunken and their mouths chiseled by grief.
Their yellow hands are the talons of an eagle.
The clamorous looms catch up the souls of the workers
And weave them into cloth;
The souls of submissive women woven into cloth;
The woman, left a husk before the loom.

Oh, the din of the mind-madding looms,
The devil-dance of the shuttles!

                        Charles Erskine Scott Wood

Our Daily Bread

On the " Hunger Parade " of the Unemployed,
Chicago, January 17, 1915.

" Give us this day our daily bread —
Give us our right," the hungry said.
Walking along the darkening way,
" Give us our daily bread," we say.

Hark to the tread of the sullen feet,
Marching down the sleety street:
Hunger staggers along the way.
" Give us our bread and work — today! "

Swaying banners overhead —
" Give us this day our daily bread."
Masses of men and women throng —
Living witness of living wrong.

" Work, not charity! " is the cry.
Is it sincere — I know not, I!
What can I give but some small dole?
But — will that satisfy my soul?

Buffeting through the wind and the rain,
They will pass again and again,
Menacing all who are sleek and fed:
" Give — or we'll take — our daily bread."

Reads like a story of long ago:
" Driven by want, driven by woe,
Peasants arose and began to slay."
But it all happened yesterday.

Reads like a tale from some far-off land,
Countries we do not understand,
  (Where there will be the devil to pay!)
But — it all happened across the way.

Rita Benton

MINE-SONG

I am the dreamless dark of the mines,
My breast filled with terrible secrets —
My silence streaked with dead men's blood!
I am fate — I am destiny to thousands
Whose lamps flicker through timbered tunnels,
Groping through caves of coal and rock.

Through endless ages I keep my stern silence,
Watching pygmies crawl through tiny holes,
Seeking the treasured coal . . .
Slaves, dropping trails of sweat as they walk,
Their lungs choked with dust,
And the dampness soaking into their feet
As they plod and dig through tight places
In my secret and terrible bosom.

O men, have you not darkness enough inside your breasts,
That you must seek it so dangerously here?
Are your nights so flung with stars
That you enter these windy caverns to flee
Their sharp beauty?

Or is it something gnawing deep inside,
Something that cannot let you rest —
Whips and stings and the pinching stomach,
Lashing and driving you up and down these dark entries,
So many helpless mules
Drawing your loads to the end of the gangway?

JUSTICE

▲

I watch you through your curses and your confusions.
I may seem to you silent and horrible —
But deep inside of me,
I laugh, and sympathize,
O brothers of the dark!

E. Falkowski

FIRES

Snug in my easy chair,
   I stirred the fire to flame.
Fantastically fair
   The flickering fancies came,
Born of heart's desire:
   Amber woodlands streaming;
   Topaz islands dreaming,
   Sunset-cities gleaming,
Spire on burning spire;
   Ruddy-windowed taverns;
Sunshine-spilling wines;
   Crystal-lighted caverns
Of Golconda's mines;
   Summers, unreturning;
   Passion's crater yearning;
   Troy, the ever-burning;
Shelley's lustral pyre;
   Dragon-eyes, unsleeping;
   Witches' cauldrons leaping;
   Golden galleys sweeping
Out from sea-walled Tyre:
   Fancies, fugitive and fair,
   Flashed with winging through the air;
   Till, dazzled by the drowsy glare,
I shut my eyes to heat and light;

And saw, in sudden night,
Crouched in the dripping dark,
With streaming shoulders stark,
The man who hews the coal to feed my fire.

Wilfrid Wilson Gibson

WE ARE THE BURDEN-BEARERS!

We are the Burden-Bearers,
   We of the bended backs;
We are the shackle-wearers,
   Stumbling the leaden tracks.

We are the mountain-makers —
   Steel-girded mountains that rise
Dwarfing the ancient Cheops,
   Into the city skies.

We are the diggers and delvers
   Under the river roof,
Tunneling granite highways;
   We are the warp and the woof.

We are the slaves of traffic
   Out where the world is new;
We are the scouts of commerce
   Cutting the pathways through.

We are the naked toilers
   Fronting the furnace flames;
We are the miracle-makers,
   Men of the nameless names.

Molten the steel about us,
   Showering sparks overhead;
Selfish the masters who flout us —
   Wounded and bleeding and dead!

▲

Over us monuments rising —
  Ours but the stress and the strain;
Towers of triumph are lifted;
  To others the glory and gain.

We are the stones of the corner;
  We the foundations of life;
We are the Burden-Bearers
  Who carry the brunt of the strife!

William L. Stidger

HAMMER AND NAILS

O Carpenter of Nazareth,
A grim true word it was You said
That night beneath the olive-shade,
That to each worker cometh death,
Too often by the tools of his own trade.

You said, O Carpenter, this hard word:
" Who takes the sword dies by the sword."
Each man by his own labor perishes:
The fisherman becomes the food of fishes;
The Carpenter is nailed upon a board.

All sailors fallen from the swaying mast,
Their bloody flesh and brains buttering the deck;
And stokers stifled by the furnace blast,
Half burned, half drowned like rats in some steel-
  stanchioned wreck.

All soldiers hanging gutted on the wire
Or firemen strangled in a noose of fire;
Masons and muckers crashing through the broken
  scaffolding

That props the palace of some careless King
Of Church or Trade;

And they who ride the smoky stallions unafraid,
Mangled and roasting in each wrecked and burning
    train;
Miners in agonizing darkness gassed
Or crushed beneath an avalanche of coal —

We pray, O Carpenter, nail-slain,
To Thee, Who knew the labor and the pain,
Be gracious to each parting soul!

But most, for our own selves we pray,
Even that we may be forgiven too
For these we slay by night and day,
Although we know well what we do.

Kenneth W. Porter

THE HUNGRY

Whom does He love the most —
    The poor, the sick, the blind,
The rich, the maimed, the host
    Unknowingly unkind?

The ones who strive, and fail;
    The ones who have, and lose;
The ones who will not quail
    Nor martyrdom refuse?

The wind went sobbing low
    To His great Heart and cried;
" Dear God, they need you so —
    Who die unsatisfied."

Caroline Giltinan

LAUGHTER

The Autumn sun is shining, round and gay,
    Above my garden, and I hear the low
    Sweet laughter of the flowering things. "Yo ho!"
They cry. "The world is beautiful today!"
    Rose-hedges circle all the smiling space
Of suave, green lawns, and gaudy flower-beds.
"The world is beautiful" . . . They toss their heads,
    And fling their perfumed beauty in my face.

But there are people at my garden gate
    Upon whose foreheads are the jagged fears
Which have companioned them; and sullen hate
    Plays on their lips, and smolders where the tears
Long since have drowned the laughter in their eyes.
"Yo ho!" they say. "Your laughing garden lies!"

Mary Craig Sinclair

THE DEVIL'S AUCTION

The Devil's auction:
The daughters of the Poor for sale.
Three dollars a week; three-and-a-half;
Four, five; five-and-a-half.
The innocent young mothers
Sold at the Devil's auction.
Eyes more precious than agates,
Chalcedony or sapphires,
Shining pools of the evening,
Wherein the stars dance,
And under the fringe of the border
Runs a liquid moon.
Cheeks more delicate than the wild-rose
Of the canyons;

JUSTICE

Bosoms pure as pond-lilies
Swaying on ripples.
Lips dewy as Aurora new bathed
In the flattery of orient seas.
My sisters, my trusting little sisters,
Shall you not snatch at roses
Drooping heavy for the picking?
Shall you not walk in the poppied paths?
Shall you be hungry and taste not of the grapes?

Charles Erskine Scott Wood

AT THE WORKERS' BENCHES

The great machines go whirling around.
Ears burst open in the buzzing sound.
Eyes look out on a world of wheels.
Master, Master, my head reels.

The air is filled with dust that lifts
Like dark clouds — and the sunlight sifts
Upon the rack where my body wrenches.
Master, come to the workers' benches.

Master, come and heal these broken thumbs.
The darkness lifts, for the Master comes.
" I once walked here with living men
And I shall walk with them again."

Raymond Kresensky

COMRADE JESUS

I tramped the pavement, cursing God,
When there beside me Jesus trod!

Now we shall walk, my Friend and I,
Across the earth, the sea, the sky.

I do not know what He may be;
I only know He walks with me.

From Eden barred and Paradise,
Too wisely sad, too sadly wise!

Oh, lonely feet!   Oh, bleeding feet!
In step with mine on city street!

Ralph Cheyney

CHRIST IN THE STREET

He came to earth one blue-skied day —
    He walked with world-men down the street:
The people stared in a wide-eyed way,
    Noting his wounded hands and feet.

Then they whispered and hurried by:
    Some of them mockingly jibed and smiled
When he stopped where buildings towered high
    To stroke the head of a ragged child.

" Out of the way," the world-men cried;
    " Hurry along," called one in blue:
" You look like a man we crucified,
    " But no . . . Oh, no . . . it was not you! "

" Have you the price of board and bed? "
    They hurled at him as nightfall neared,
And when he shook his thorn-scourged head
    The mob pressed close and laughed and jeered.

" Have you a house of bricks? " they called,
    " Or a chariot which runs alone —
A vault for silver, steeled and walled
    With blocks of mighty granite stone? "

▲

" Have you some other earth-made thing —
   A purse of coins or flying plane?
You who have called yourself a king —
   You must have prospered through your reign."

The night closed in — none gave a crust:
   I heard the wan Christ groan and say:
" Better my dark tomb in the dust
   Than the world today . . . than men today."

Jay G. Sigmund

COMRADE JESUS

Thanks to Saint Matthew, who had been
At mass-meetings in Palestine,
We know whose side was spoken for
When Comrade Jesus had the floor.

" Where sore they toiled and hard they lie,
Among the great unwashed dwell I —
The tramp, the convict, I am he;
Cold-shoulder him, cold-shoulder me."

By Dives' door, with thoughtful eye,
He did tomorrow prophesy:
" The kingdom's gate is low and small;
The rich can scarce wedge through at all."

" A dangerous man," said Caiaphas;
" An ignorant demagogue, alas!
Friend of low women, it is he
Slanders the upright Pharisee."

For law and order, it was plain,
For Holy Church, he must be slain.
The troops were there to awe the crowd,
And violence was not allowed.

[172]

▲

Their clumsy force with force to foil
His strong, clean hands he would not soil.
He saw their childishness quite plain
Between the lightnings of his pain.

Between the twilights of his end,
He made his fellow-felon friend;
With swollen tongue and blinding eyes,
Invited him to Paradise.

Ah, let no local him refuse!
Comrade Jesus hath paid his dues.
Whatever other be debarred,
Comrade Jesus hath his red card.

Sarah N. Cleghorn

THE COMMON STREET

The common street climbed up against the sky,
Gray meeting gray; and wearily to and fro
I saw the patient, common people go,
Each with his sordid burden trudging by.
And the rain dropped; there was not any sigh
Or stir of a live wind; dull, dull and slow
All motion; as a tale told long ago
The faded world; and creeping night drew nigh.
Then burst the sunset, flooding far and fleet,
Leavening the whole of life with magic leaven.
Suddenly down the long wet glistening hill
Pure splendor poured — and lo! the common street,
A golden highway into golden heaven,
With the dark shapes of men ascending still.

Helen Gray Cone

CITY COMRADESHIP

Face on face in the city, and when will the faces end?
Face on face in the city, but never the face of a friend;
Till my heart grows sick with longing and dazed with
　　the din of the street,
As I rush with the thronging thousands in a loneliness
　　complete.

Shall I not know my brothers?　Their toil is one with
　　mine.
We offer the fruits of our labor on the same great city's
　　shrine.
They are weary as I am weary; they are happy and sad
　　with me;
And all of us laugh together when evening sets us free.

Face on face in the city, and where shall our fortunes
　　fall?
Face on face in the city — my heart goes out to you all.
See, we labor together; is not the bond divine?
Lo! the strength of the city is built of your life and mine.

Anna Louise Strong

VOICES

Voices, voices, they call to me:
" Here to the left."　" There to the right."
" Go up the hill where you can see
The face of peace in a glow of light."

" Go, take your visions high in the air
And set your banner on a cloud.
Forget old men and their despair;
Forget, and go with head unbowed."

"Go with your brothers down the slope,
Humble and bowed to meet the test,
Where men in darkness faint and grope
Lacking the peace of hope and rest."

Voices, voices, they call to me.
One voice of all comes back again,
Calling, calling incessantly:
"Walk in the vale with suffering men."

Raymond Kresensky

GOD'S PITY

God pity all the brave who go
  The common way, and wear
No ribboned medals on their breasts,
  No laurels in their hair.

God pity all the lonely folk
  With griefs they do not tell,
Women waking in the night
  And men dissembling well.

In common courage of the street
  The crushed grape is the wine,
Wheat in the mill is daily bread
  And given for a sign.

And who but God shall pity those
  Who go so quietly
And smile upon us when we meet
  And greet so pleasantly.

Louise Driscoll

The Touch of Human Hands

The touch of human hands —
That is the boon we ask;
For groping, day by day,
Along the stony way,
We need the comrade heart
That understands,
And the warmth, the pulsing warmth
Of human hands.

The touch of human hands —
Not vain, unthinking words,
Nor that cold charity
Which shuns our misery;
We seek a loyal friend
Who understands,
And the warmth, the loving warmth
Of human hands.

The touch of human hands —
Such care as was in Him
Who walked in Galilee
Beside the silver sea;
We need a patient guide
Who understands,
And the warmth, the living warmth
Of human hands.

Thomas Curtis Clark

PICCADILLY

Beautiful, tragical faces —
Ye that were whole, and are so sunken;
And, O ye vile, ye that might have been loved,
That are so sodden and drunken,
   Who hath forgotten you?

O wistful, fragile faces, few out of many!
The crass, the coarse, the brazen,
God knows I cannot pity them, perhaps, as I should do;
But oh, ye delicate, wistful faces,
   Who hath forgotten you?

Ezra Pound

ROSES IN THE SUBWAY

A wan-cheeked girl with faded eyes
   Came stumbling down the crowded car,
Clutching her burden to her breast
   As though she held a star.

Roses, I swear it! Red and sweet
   And struggling from her pinched white hands,
Roses . . . like captured hostages
   From far and fairy lands!

The thunder of the rushing train
   Was like a hush. . . . The flower scent
Breathed faintly on the stale, whirled air
   Like some dim sacrament —

I saw a garden stretching out
   And morning on it like a crown —
And o'er a bed of crimson bloom
   My mother . . . stooping down.

Dana Burnet

THE CHILD

You may be Christ or Shakespeare, little child,
A savior or a sun to the lost world —
There is no babe born but may carry furled
Strength to make bloom the world's disastrous wild!
Oh, what then must our labors be to mold you,
To open the heart, to build with dream the brain,
To strengthen the young soul in toil and pain,
Till our age-aching hands no longer hold you —

Vision far-dreamed! — But soft! if your last goal
Be low, if you are only common clay —
What then? Toil lost? Were our toil trebled, nay!
You are a Soul, you are a human Soul,
A greater than the skies by star-hosts trod,
Shakespeare no greater, O you slip of God!

James Oppenheim

REALIZATION

Into the woods I wandered,
   One said, " God is there."
Hours and hours I squandered,
   Questioning, " Where, where? "

I strayed to the slums of a city;
   A child in rags drew near
And fed the birds from pity.
   I whispered, " God is here."

Beth Cheney-Nichols

[178]

▲

STREETS OF GOLD

I hope that the streets of Heaven
   Are not encased with gold —
They would be cruel for the crippled,
   The baby feet, and old.

They would be blinding and searing
   To washer-women come
Out of the steaming cellars
   Hid in the city slum.

They would be bound to blister
   The swollen half-naked feet
That sought for work through the city,
   In harrowing cold, and heat.

I pray that the seraphs will carpet
   Heaven's highways with evergreen grass —
Scented, dew-drenched in the morning,
   Cool for the feet that pass.

Earl Bigelow Brown

THE DREAM-BEARER

Where weary folk toil, black with smoke,
   And hear but whistles scream,
I went, all fresh from dawn and dew,
   To carry them a dream.

I went to bitter lanes and dark,
   Who once had known the sky,
To carry them a dream — and found
   They had more dreams than I.

Mary Carolyn Davies

[179]

JUDGE NOT

Written in prison

A wreck? Who gave you right to judge? Oh, shame,
    What know you of the iron street he trod?
How dare you place Defeat against his name,
    Are you the mouthpiece of Almighty God?

Are you the keeper of the judgment scroll,
    The book wherein is writ God's awful lore?
Silence! Each man is captain of his soul,
    And captain he till God adds up the score.

                    John Francis Glynn

SIMON THE CYRENIAN SPEAKS

He never spoke a word to me
And yet He called my name.
He never gave a sign to me
And yet I knew and came.

At first I said, "I will not bear
This load upon my back —
He only means to place it there
Because my skin is black."

But He was dying for a dream,
And He was very meek;
And in His eyes there shone a gleam
Men journey far to seek.

It was Himself my pity brought;
I did for Christ alone
What all of Rome could not have wrought
With bruise of lash or stone.

                    Countee Cullen

JUSTICE FOR WOMANKIND

Slowly the gates of opportunity
  Open at last, and ever more and more
Woman is ruler of her destiny
  And shattered many a bond that once she bore.
All shall be broken! Man shall seek her aid,
  Not in the narrow bounds of home alone,
But for the common weal, and wife and maid
  Shall speak with voice as potent as his own.
God speed the moment when in every land
All doors shall open to a woman's hand!

William Dudley Foulke

BLIND

He saw the noonday sun,
The shadow cast by trees,
The distant hills in blue veils run,
The women weeding on their knees,
The sweaty plowman close behind,
And yet the man who saw was blind.

He saw the twilight come,
The lights flash in the streets,
Thousands hurrying from the hum
Of great machines, the roar that beats
Into the heart and brain of humankind,
And yet the man who saw was blind.

· · · · ·

He saw the starving world,
He never met the need,
The great god Greed had always whirled

▲

The dust and blotted out the seed
That might have blossomed in his mind,
He did not know that he was blind!

June Lucas

Prayer for Spring

Let the spring sun creep close to those.
  Whose lives are sealed in winter pain,
Let them find courage in the skies
  And blessings in the rain!

Let spring flash by where women toil
  Whose flesh has burned on travail bed
And who have closed in tearless grief
  The eyelids of the dead!

Let the spring come when men shall walk
  New hills with kindness in their eyes,
When comrade hearts shall beat as one
  Beneath emancipated skies.

Sylvia Hill

To a Student

Let crowded city pavements be your school,
  Your text, the varied faces that you see,
An understanding heart and mind, your tool,
  The art of human kindness your degree.

E. K. Biddle

RENUNCIATION

Give me the crown of thorns; let fair and sweet
The roses in the garden bloom;
Bedeck me not with garlands lest my feet
Should stumble 'neath the dense perfume,
And scarlet petals crushing stain the garments of my
     soul.

Give me the crown of thorns; the stately bay
Can only mighty brows adorn,
Of souls that shine as stars along the way.
Bestow on me the barren thorn,
To wait its chancing verdure as it pierces to my soul.

Fanny Bixby Spencer

PRIDE

" We are proud of death," Sacco said.
But better to be living than be dead.

Yes, proud of death; and death should be proud, too,
Proud of these men that Justice slew.

But death is far too proud. She'd rather give
Them back to life, and let them live!

Henry Harrison

THE RULERS

The world is led by men whom it has slain.
They are its mighty rulers. Unharmed Christ
Would not have conquered millions. Once again
We watch while innocence is sacrificed.

Release them, and you leave them men, but slay them —
And unborn millions some day may obey them.

Mary Carolyn Davies

FAILURES

Salute, if you will, pioneers of the air,
Men who with courage face death and despair,
Heroes of science who vanquish the sky,
Give them their honor, salute them — but I,
I shall sing of the failures, defeated, alone,
Who knew how men suffer and heard how men moan,
Whose pity was vast and whose faith could remain
Through all the world's mocking and savage disdain,
Men with dreams of tomorrow and deeds of today,
Sacco, Vanzetti, Gene Debs and Jaures!
Hail men who conquer material goals,
I shall sing of the martyrs who conquer men's souls.

Lucia Trent

MOURN NOT THE DEAD

Mourn not the dead that in the cool earth lie —
Dust unto dust —
The calm sweet earth that mothers all who die
As all men must;

Mourn not your captured comrades who must dwell —
Too strong to strive —
Each in his steel-bound coffin of a cell,
Buried alive;

But rather mourn the apathetic throng —
The cowed and the meek —
Who see the world's great anguish and its wrong
And dare not speak!

Ralph Chaplin

JUSTICE

▲

They Are All for You

When the psalm sings instead of the singer;
When the script preaches instead of the preacher;
When the pulpit descends and goes, instead of the carver
    that carved the supporting desk;
When I can touch the body of books, by night or by
    day, and when they touch my body back again;
When a university course convinces, like a slumbering
    woman and child convince;
When the minted gold in the vault smiles like the night
    watchman's daughter;
When warrantee deeds loaf in chairs opposite, and are
    my friendly companions;
I intend to reach them my hand, and make as much of
    them as I do of men and women like you.
The sum of all known reverence I add up in you, who-
    ever you are;
The President is there in the White House for you — it
    is not you who are here for him;
The Secretaries act in their bureaus for you — not you
    here for them;
The Congress convenes every Twelfth-month for you;
Laws, courts, the forming of States, the charters of cities,
    the going and coming of commerce and mails, are
    all for you.
All music is what awakes from you when you are re-
    minded by the instruments;
It is not the violins and the cornets — it is not the oboe
    nor the beating drums, nor the score of the bari-
    tone singer singing his sweet romanza — nor that
    of the men's chorus, nor that of the women's chorus,
It is nearer and farther than they.

Walt Whitman

From " Carol of Occupations "

[185]

The God of the Social Passion

Forgive, dear God, that we have sought Thy face
Elsewhere than in these human faces dear,
That our cold heart has thought to win Thy grace
Save in their conquering smile, atoning tear.

The throne vain fancy sets above the skies,
Transcendencies our pompous schemes essay —
Before the holy light of human eyes
Flooding our souls, the shadows flee away;

And when we claim Thee human, then we find
Not less, but ever more and more of Thee —
Exhaustless thought with simplest task entwined —
Deepest because the Closest mystery.

Author Unknown

God's Dreams

Dreams are they — but they are God's dreams!
Shall we decry them and scorn them?
That men shall love one another,
That white shall call black man brother,
That greed shall pass from the market-place,
That lust shall yield to love for the race,
That man shall meet with God face to face —
Dreams are they all,
   But shall we despise them —
      God's dreams!

Dreams are they — to become man's dreams!
Can we say nay as they claim us?
That men shall cease from their hating,
That war shall soon be abating,

That the glory of kings and lords shall pale,
That the pride of dominion and power shall fail,
That the love of humanity shall prevail —
Dreams are they all,
    But shall we despise them —
        God's dreams!

Thomas Curtis Clark

CONFESSION

Once I made a political creed out of justice to the down-
    trodden,
And swore that I would rather consort with prostitutes
    and pimps,
With the ignorant and the criminal,
Outcast and the oppressed . . .
Not knowing, of course,
That I was moved, not by a love of Truth and of Justice,
But by a love of self . . .
For my self was low and belonged among the low,
And I hid the fact
By thinking I was one of the great and high
Overflowing with brotherly love.

James Oppenheim

From " The Book of Self "

From PRAIRIE

O prairie mother, I am one of your boys.
I have loved the prairie as a man with a heart shot full
    of pain over love.
Here I know I will hanker after nothing so much as one
    more sunrise, or a sky moon of fire doubled to a
    river moon of water.

J U S T I C E

I speak of new cities and new people.
I tell you the past is a bucket of ashes.
I tell you yesterday is a wind gone down,
        A sun dropped in the west.
I tell you there is nothing in the world
        Only an ocean of tomorrows,
        A sky of tomorrows.

I am a brother of the cornhuskers who say at sundown:
        Tomorrow is a day.

Carl Sandburg

Voice

You in whose veins runs the fire of loving,
For people, for plants, for little animals,
For rocks and earth, stars and the elements,
You have a secret Voice, always singing.
It is never still. It runs with your haste
And idles in your silence. It is everywhere.
O you, for whom this passionate Voice sings
And will not be silent, think now of those
For whom no voice sounds. Of those who toil
Without the singing voice,
And live in a world which has not yet come through
Into your world.
Oh, can you not hear that the song your Voice is singing
Is the song which is to bring that world of theirs
Into the light which must light all men?

Why else do you imagine that this Voice is singing?
Why else do you imagine that the fire of love
Runs in your veins?

Zona Gale

[188]

The Innocent Ones Who Come After

O God, we pray Thee for those who come after us, for
our children, and the children of our friends, and
for all the young lives that are marching up from
the gates of birth, pure and eager, with the morning
sunshine on their faces. We remember with a pang
that these will live in the world we are making for
them. We are wasting the resources of the earth
in our headlong greed, and they will suffer want.
We are building sunless houses and joyless cities for
our profit, and they must dwell therein. We are
making the burden heavy and the pace of work
pitiless, and they will fall wan and sobbing by the
wayside. We are poisoning the air of our land by
our lies and our uncleanness, and they will breathe
it.

O God, thou knowest how we have cried out in agony
when the sins of our fathers have been visited upon
us, and how we have struggled vainly against the
inexorable fate that coursed in our blood or bound
us in a prison-house of life. Save us from maiming
the innocent ones who come after us by the added
cruelty of our sins. Help us to break the ancient
force of evil by a holy and steadfast will and to
endow our children with purer blood and nobler
thoughts.

Grant us grace to leave the earth fairer than we found
it; to build upon it cities of God in which the cry
of needless pain shall cease; and to put the yoke of
Christ upon our business life that it may serve and
not destroy.

Lift the veil of the future and show us the generation to
come as it will be if blighted by our guilt, that our

lust may be cooled and we may walk in the fear of
the Eternal.
Grant us a vision of the far-off years as they may be if
redeemed by the sons of God, that we may take
heart and do battle for thy children and ours.

Walter Rauschenbusch

IF HE SHOULD COME

If Jesus should tramp the streets tonight,
  Storm-beaten and hungry for bread,
Seeking a room and a candle light
  And a clean though humble bed,
Who would welcome the Workman in,
  Though He came with panting breath,
His hands all bruised and His garments thin —
  This Workman from Nazareth?

Would rich folk hurry to bind His bruise
  And shelter His stricken form?
Would they take God in with His muddy shoes
  Out of the pitiless storm?
Are they not too busy wreathing their flowers
  Or heaping their golden store —
Too busy chasing the bubble hours
  For the poor man's God at the door?

And if He should come where churchmen bow,
  Forgetting the greater sin,
Would He pause with a light on His wounded brow,
  Would He turn and enter in?
And what would He think of their creeds so dim,
  Of their weak, uplifted hands,
Of their selfish prayers going up to Him
  Out of a thousand lands?

Edwin Markham

POEMS OF
JUSTICE

▲▲▲▲▲▲▲▲▲▲▲▲▲

DREAMS AND
GOALS

▼

From PIONEERS! O PIONEERS!

Have the elder races halted?
Do they droop and end their lesson, wearied, over there
    beyond the seas?
We take up the task eternal, and the burden, and the
    lesson,
      Pioneers! O Pioneers!

All the past we leave behind;
We debouch upon a newer, mightier world, varied
    world;
Fresh and strong the world we seize, world of labor and
    the march,
      Pioneers! O Pioneers!

We detachments steady throwing,
Down the edges, through the passes, up the mountains
    steep,
Conquering, holding, daring, venturing, as we go, the
    unknown ways,
      Pioneers! O Pioneers!

    .   .   .   .   .

See, my children, resolute children,
By those swarms upon our rear, we must never yield or
    falter,
Ages back in ghostly millions, frowning there behind
    us urging,
      Pioneers! O Pioneers!

On and on, the compact ranks,
With accessions ever waiting, with the places of the
 dead quickly filled,
Through the battle, through defeat, moving yet and
 never stopping,
  Pioneers! O Pioneers!

Oh, to die advancing on!
Are there some of us to droop and die? Has the hour
 come?
Then upon the march we fittest die, soon and sure the
 gap is filled,
  Pioneers! O Pioneers!

All the pulses of the world,
Falling in, they beat for us, with the western movement
 beat;
Holding single or together, steady moving, to the front,
 all for us,
  Pioneers! O Pioneers!

. . . . . .

Has the night descended?
Was the road of late so toilsome? did we stop dis-
 couraged, nodding on our way?
Yet a passing hour I yield you, in your tracks to pause
 oblivious,
  Pioneers! O Pioneers!

Till with sound of trumpet,
Far, far off the daybreak call — hark! how loud and
 clear I hear it wind;
Swift! to the head of the army! — swift! spring to your
 places,
  Pioneers! O Pioneers!

Walt Whitman

The Spirit of Brotherhood

The law of God is one, as God is one; but we only discover it article by article, line by line.

We can only rise to God through the souls of our fellowmen.

God is in you without doubt; but God is likewise in all men who people this earth;

God is in the life of all generations which were, which are, and which are to be.

God has given you the general opinion of your fellowmen, and your own conscience, to be to you two wings with which to soar to Him.

God asks not what have you done for your soul? but what have you done for the brother souls I gave you?

Wherever a man suffers through the oppression of error, of injustice, of tyranny, there is your brother.

Why speak of Brotherhood and yet allow our brothers every day to be trampled, degraded, despised?

If error rules your brothers in some other corner of this earth and you do not desire, and endeavor as far as lies in your power, to overthrow it, you are false to your duty.

A solemn mission is ours: to prove that we are all sons of God and brothers in Him.

Joseph Mazzini

A Confession of Faith

I believe in God, who is for me spirit, love, the principle of all things.

I believe that God is in me, as I am in Him.

I believe that the true welfare of man consists in fulfilling the will of God.

I believe that from the fulfilment of the will of God there can follow nothing but that which is good for me and for all men.

I believe that the will of God is that every man should love his fellowmen, and should act toward others as he desires that they should act toward him.

I believe that the reason of life is for each of us simply to grow in love.

I believe that this growth in love will contribute more than any other force to establish the Kingdom of God on earth —

To replace a social life in which division, falsehood and violence are all-powerful, with a new order in which humanity, truth and brotherhood will reign.

Leo Tolstoy

From " My Religion "

In the Deep Caves of the Heart

In the deep caves of the heart, far down, running under the outward shows of the world and of people,
Running under continents, under the fields and the roots of the grasses and trees,

[196]

Under the little thoughts and dreams of men, and the
    history of races,
I see, feel and hear wondrous and divine things.
I seem to see the strands of affection and love, so tender,
    so true and life-long, holding together the present
    and past generations.
The currents of love and thought streaming in the
    watches of the night from far and near, from one
    to another,
Streaming all the more powerfully for the very hin-
    drances and disasters which arrive or threaten.
I dream that these are the fibers and nerves of a body
    that lies within the outer body of society;
A network, an innumerable vast interlocked ramifica-
    tion, slowly being built up;
All dear lovers and friends, all families, groups, all
    peoples, nations, all times, all worlds perhaps,
Members of a body, archetypal, eterne, glorious, the
    center and perfection of life.
The organic growth of God Himself in time.

Edward Carpenter

From " Towards Democracy "

BREAKING THE MOLDS

We are breaking up the molds
With a rattle and a clatter,
Wielding hammers at strongholds,
Laughing as the fragments scatter,
And our hands, once brave for making,
Tear and hurl and crash and batter,
With a frenzy in the breaking,
And a passion that shall shatter

All the molds,
The ancient molds,
In this white hour of our waking.

So we swing the hammers high,
Braces yield and walls grow slack,
Spires topple from the sky,
Roof-trees massive, chimneys black,
Mosque and temple, shop and jail,
Make a litter like the sack
Of a town in some old tale,
When the molds begin to crack,
All the molds,
The ancient molds,
Weighed and wanting in the scale.

But a new world shall be won,
That no hand shall smite or tear —
So we cry, who stumble, run,
Hammers lifted, while we spare
One small mold — two feet, two hands,
And a round head hot with hair!
This the mold that scars and brands
With its flaw, what worlds we dare!
This the mold,
The ancient mold,
That yields and bends and cracks — but stands.

We are breaking up the molds
With a rattle and a clatter,
Wielding hammers at strongholds,
Laughing as the fragments scatter,
Singing as our chisels gnaw,
Biting through the stones we shatter,
Breaking without rule or law —

Molds must go — it does not matter —
All the molds,
The ancient molds,
Shaped of one mold with a flaw!

Hortense Flexner

THE DEAR LOVE OF COMRADES

I hear it is charged against me that I seek to destroy
    institutions;
But really I am neither for nor against institutions,
(What indeed have I in common with them? — Or
    what with the destruction of them?)
Only I will establish in the Mannahatta, and in every
    city of these States, inland and seaboard,
And in the fields and woods, and above every keel little
    or large, that dents the water,
Without edifices, or rules, or trustees, or any argument,
The institution of the dear love of comrades.

Walt Whitman

From " Calamus "

THE DAY IS COMING

Come hither, lads, and hearken,
for a tale there is to tell,
Of the wonderful days a-coming,
when all shall be better than well.

And the tale shall be told of a country,
a land in the midst of the sea,
And folk shall call it England
in the days that are going to be.

▲

There more than one in a thousand
in the days that are yet to come,
Shall have some hope of the morrow
some joy of the ancient home.

For then, laugh not, but listen
to this strange tale of mine,
All folk that are in England
shall be better lodged than swine.

Then a man shall work and bethink him
and rejoice in the deeds of his hand,
Nor yet come home in the even
too faint and weary to stand.

Men in that time a-coming
shall work and have no fear
For to-morrow's lack of earning
and the hunger-wolf anear.

I tell you this for a wonder,
that no man then shall be glad
Of his fellow's fall and mishap
to snatch at the work he had.

For that which the worker winneth
shall then be his indeed,
Nor shall half be reaped for nothing
by him that sowed no seed.

Oh, strange new wonderful justice!
But for whom shall we gather the gain?
For ourselves and for each of our fellows,
and no hand shall labor in vain.

Then all Mine and all Thine shall be Ours,
and no more shall any man crave

For riches that serve for nothing
but to fetter a friend for a slave.

And what wealth then shall be left us
when none shall gather gold
To buy his friend in the market,
and pinch and pine the sold?

Nay, what save the lovely city,
and the little house on the hill,
And the wastes and the woodland beauty,
and the happy fields we till;

And the homes of ancient stories,
the tombs of the mighty dead;
And the wise men seeking out marvels,
and the poet's teeming head;

And the painter's hand of wonder;
and the marvelous fiddle-bow;
And the banded choirs of music:
all those that do and know.

For all these shall be ours and all men's,
nor shall any lack a share
Of the toil and the gain of living
in the days when the world grows fair.

William Morris

BROTHERHOOD

There shall rise from this confused sound of voices
    A firmer faith than that our fathers knew,
A deep religion which alone rejoices
    In worship of the Infinitely True,
Not built on rite or portent, but a finer
And purer reverence for a Lord diviner.

JUSTICE

▲

There shall come from out this noise of strife and
    groaning
  A broader and a juster brotherhood,
A deep equality of aim, postponing
  All selfish seeking to the general good.
There shall come a time when each shall to another
Be as Christ would have him — brother unto brother.

There shall come a time when knowledge, wide extended,
  Seeks each man's pleasure in the general health,
And all shall hold irrevocably blended
  The individual and the commonwealth;
When man and woman in an equal union
Shall merge, and marriage be a true communion.

There shall come a time when brotherhood shows
    stronger
Than the narrow bounds which now distract the world,
When the cannon's roar and trumpets blare no longer,
And the ironclad rusts, and battle flags are furled;
When the bars of creed and speech and race, which sever,
Shall be fused in one humanity forever.

Lewis Morris

THE DREAMER

I hail you, " Dreamers "! I pick you out of the crowd,
Out of the surging multitude, that fancies its noise is
    Life;
Dreamers? must a man be asleep because he cries not
    aloud;
Is the worth of a man discovered by the force that he
    gives to strife?

I know you, Dreamers; your cloaks are frayed by the
wind;
Empty your scrips; for when did a Dreamer barter for
gold his soul?
I know by the way ye stumble on, as if ye were gropers
blind;
For why should a dreamer mind the earth, when his eyes
have stars for the goal?

I know you, Dreamers; I know by the tongue ye speak;
The tongue which none but Dreamers and Seraphs may
ever aspire to learn;
I know by the gleam of the ghost-light in eyes that are
strong yet meek;
By the light on your cheeks and lips where the cleansing
Seer-coals burn.

I bless you, Dreamers! Oh, wonder not if men jeer;
Was ever a prophet given aught but the scourgers' rod?
If dreamers ye be, ah, Dreamers, would that we, too,
might peer
Into that sleep where the earth-free soul is face to face
with its God.

Hugh Francis Blunt

Sound Over All Waters

Sound over all waters, reach out from all lands, the
chorus of voices, the clasping of hands;
Sing hymns that were sung by the stars of the morn;
sing songs of the angels when Jesus was born!
With glad jubilations bring hope to the nations!
The dark night is ending and dawn has begun; rise, hope
of the ages, arise like the sun.
All speech flow to music, all hearts beat as one!

Sing the bridal of nations! with chorals of love; sing out
the war vultures and sing in the dove.
Till the hearts of the peoples keep time in accord, and
the voice of the world is the voice of the Lord!
Clasp hands of the nations in strong gratulations;
The dark night is ending and dawn has begun;
Rise, hope of the ages, arise like the sun, all speech flow
to music, all hearts beat as one!

Blow, bugle of battle, the marches of peace; east, west,
north and south, let the long quarrel cease;
Sing the song of great joy that the angels began, sing of
glory to God and of good-will to man!
Hark! joining in chorus the heavens bend o'er us!
The dark night is ending and dawn has begun;
Rise, hope of the ages, arise like the sun, all speech flow
to music, all hearts beat as one.

Stanton Coit

CHILDREN OF TOMORROW

Come, Children of Tomorrow, come!
New glory dawns upon the world.
The ancient banners must be furled.
The earth becomes our common home —
The earth becomes our common home.
From plain and field and town there sound
The stirring rumors of the day.
Old wrongs and burdens must make way
For men to tread the common ground.

Look up! The children win to their immortal place.
March on, march on — within the ranks of all the
human race.

Come, love of people, for the part
Invest our willing arms with might!
Mother of Liberty, shed light
As on the land, so in the heart —
As on the land, so in the heart.
Divided we have long withstood
The love that is our common speech.
The comrade cry of each to each
Is calling us to humanhood.

Zona Gale

FOR THE NEW AGE

The sound of anthems rarer grows and faint:
Shamed in his robes is many a mummering priest.
How empty now the sacerdotal feast —
Mere bread, mere wine, rises the vague complaint.
Now wider spread the canker and the taint
Of social woes by putrid creeds increased;
Loud grow the jeers of those once called the least
'Gainst pomp and panoply and crusted paint.

But underneath the tumult and the moan,
Beyond the jarring blows at Time's slow door,
God's groping orchestra cons o'er and o'er
That mightier music no man e'er has known.
Be calm, my soul, for soon the bell chimes clear
That all may know — the Better Days draw near!

Richard Warner Borst

AS A STRONG BIRD ON PINIONS FREE

Beautiful World of new, superber Birth, that rises to
my eyes,
Like a limitless golden cloud, filling the western sky. . . .

JUSTICE

▲

Thou Wonder World, yet undefined, unformed —
    neither do I define thee;
How can I pierce the impenetrable blank of the future?
I feel thy ominous greatness, evil as well as good;
I watch thee, advancing, absorbing the present, tran-
    scending the past;
I see thy light lighting and thy shadow shadowing, as if
    the entire globe;
But I do not undertake to define thee — hardly to com-
    prehend thee;
I but thee name — thee prophesy — as now!

Walt Whitman

A Nation's Strength

What makes a nation's pillars high
    And its foundations strong?
What makes it mighty to defy
    The foes that round it throng?

It is not gold. Its kingdoms grand
    Go down in battle shock;
Its shafts are laid on sinking sand,
    Not on abiding rock.

Is it the sword? Ask the red dust
    Of empires passed away;
The blood has turned their stones to rust,
    Their glory to decay.

And is it pride? Ah, that bright crown
    Has seemed to nations sweet;
But God has struck its luster down
    In ashes at his feet.

Not gold but only men can make
  A people great and strong;
Men who for truth and honor's sake
  Stand fast and suffer long.

Brave men who work while others sleep,
  Who dare while others fly —
They build a nation's pillars deep
  And lift them to the sky.

Ralph Waldo Emerson

From PRESENTIMENT OF BETTER THINGS

We rest in faith that man's perfection is the crowning
  flower, towards which the urgent sap in life's great
  tree is pressing — seen in puny blossoms now,
But in the world's great morrows to expand with
  broadest petal and with deepest glow,
The faith that life on earth is being shaped to glorious
  ends.
Full souls are double mirrors, making still an endless
  vista of fair things before, repeating things behind.
So faith is strong only when we are strong, shrinks when
  we shrink.
It comes when music stirs us, and the chords, moving on
  some grand climax, shake our souls with influx new
  that makes new energies.
It comes in swellings of the heart and tears that rise at
  noble and at gentle deeds.
At labors of the master-artist's hand, which, trembling,
  touches to a finer end, trembling before an image
  seen within.
It comes in moments of heroic love, unjealous joy in joy

not made for us — in conscious triumph of the good
within, making us worship goodness that rebukes.

Even our failures are a prophecy, even our yearnings and
our bitter tears after that fair and true we cannot
grasp;

As patriots who seem to die in vain make liberty more
sacred by their pangs.

Presentiment of better things on earth sweep in with
every force that stirs our souls to admiration.

Self-renouncing love, or thoughts, like light, that bind
the world in one:

Sweeps like the sense of vastness, when at night we hear
the roll and dash of waves that break nearer and
nearer with the rushing tide,

Which rises to the level of the cliff because the wide
Atlantic rolls behind, throbbing respondent to the
far-off orbs.

George Eliot

Years of the Unperformed

Years of the unperformed! your horizon rises — oh, see
it parting away for more august dramas;

I see not America only — I see not only Liberty's nation,
but other nations preparing;

I see tremendous entrances and exits — I see new com-
binations — I see the solidarity of races;

I see that force advancing with irresistible power on the
world's stage;

. . . . .

I see men marching and counter-marching by swift
millions;

I see the frontiers and boundaries of the old aristocracies
broken;

I see the landmarks of European kings removed;
I see this day the People beginning their landmarks,
(all others give way);
Never were such sharp questions asked as this day;
Never was average man, his soul, more energetic, more
like God;

. . . . .

The earth, restive, confronts a new era;
No one knows what will happen next — such portents
fill the days and nights;
Years prophetical; the space ahead is full of phantoms;
Unborn deeds, things soon to be, project their shapes
around me;
This incredible rush and heat — this strange ecstatic
fever of dreams, O years!
Your dreams, O years, how they penetrate through me!
(I know not whether I sleep or wake.)
The performed America and Europe grow dim, retiring
in the shadow behind me,
The unperformed, more gigantic than ever, advance,
advance, advance upon me.

Walt Whitman

A Nobler Order

For still the new transcends the old, in signs and tokens
manifold; slaves rise up men, the olive waves with
roots deep set in battle graves.
True word, kind deed, sweet song shall vibrate still in
rings that wander through celestial air;
And human will shall build for human will fair basement
to a palace yet more fair.
The end lies hid in future victory, won by the faithful-
ness of man to man.

Presentiment of better things on earth sweeps in with
every force that stirs our souls to admiration, self-
renouncing love.

Or thoughts, like light, that bind the world in one.

From out the throng and stress of lies, from out the
painful noise of sighs, one voice of comfort seems
to rise; " It is the meaner part that dies."

Truer church shall be than in old times, lordlier govern-
ment shall bless the nations, sweeter lips shall murmur sweeter rhymes, life shall give us holier revelations.

Then shall all shackles fall; the stormy clangor of wild
war music o'er the earth shall cease;

Love shall tread out the baleful fire of anger, and in its
ashes plant the tree of peace.

Then shall the devout rejoice, and the profane shall
mourn.

Then shall he more rejoice that hath beat down his own
flesh, than he that hath abounded in all pleasure
and delight.

Then shall the poor attire shine gloriously, and the
precious robes seem vile and contemptible.

Then shall be more commended the poor cottage than
the gilded palace.

Then shall a good and clear conscience more rejoice a
man than the learning of philosophy.

Then shall the contempt of riches weigh more than all
the worldling's treasure.

Then will good works avail more than many goodly
words.

     .   .   .   .   .

Out of the dark the circling sphere is rounding onward
to the light; we see not yet the full day here, but
we do see the paling night.

I follow, follow, sure to meet the sun, and confident
that what the future yields, will be the right, unless
myself be wrong.

Arranged by *Stanton Coit*

Two Dwelling Places

For the finer spirits of (the world) there are two dwelling places: our earthly fatherland, and that other
City of God.

Of the one we are the guests, of the other the builders.

To the one let us give our lives and our faithful hearts;
but neither family, friend, nor fatherland has power
over the spirit.

The spirit is the light.

It is our duty to lift it above tempests, and thrust aside
the clouds which threaten to obscure it,

To build higher and stronger, dominating the injustice
and hatred of nations, the walls of that city wherein
the souls of the whole world may assemble.

Romaine Rolland

From " Above the Battle "

From Locksley Hall

Men, my brothers, men the workers, ever reaping something new:

That which they have done but earnest of the things that
they shall do:

For I dipt into the future, far as human eye could see,

Saw the Vision of the world, and all the wonder that
would be;

Saw the heavens fill with commerce, argosies of magic
sails,
Pilots of the purple twilight, dropping down with costly
bales;
Heard the heavens fill with shouting, and there rain'd a
ghastly dew
From the nations' airy navies grappling in the central
blue;
Far along the world-wide whisper of the south-wind
rushing warm,
With the standards of the peoples plunging through the
thunder-storm;
Till the war-drum throbb'd no longer, and the battle-
flags were furl'd
In the Parliament of man, the Federation of the world.
There the common sense of most shall hold a fretful
realm in awe,
And the kindly earth shall slumber, lapt in universal law.

Alfred Tennyson

CONSCRIPTS OF THE DREAM

Give thanks, O heart, for the high souls
That point us to the deathless goals —
For all the courage of their cry
That echoes down from sky to sky;
Thanksgiving for the armèd seers
And heroes called to mortal years —
Souls that have built our faith in man,
And lit the ages as they ran.

Lincoln, Mazzini, Lamennais,
Doing the deed that others pray;
Cromwell, St. Francis, and the rest,

Bearing the God-fire in the breast —
These are the sons of sacred flame,
Their brows marked with the sacred name —
The company of souls supreme,
The conscripts of the mighty Dream.

Made of unpurchasable stuff,
They went the way when ways were rough:
They, when the traitors had deceived,
Held the long purpose, and believed:
They, when the face of God grew dim,
Held through the dark and trusted Him —
Brave souls that took the perilous trail
And felt the vision could not fail.

Give thanks for heroes who have stirred
Earth with the wonder of a word.
But all thanksgiving for the breed
Who have bent destiny with deed —
Souls of the high, heroic birth,
Souls sent to poise the shaken Earth,
And then called back to God again
To make Heaven possible for men.

Edwin Markham

SONG OF THE NEW WORLD

I sing the song of a new Dawn waking,
   A new wind shaking the children of men.
I say the hearts that are nigh to breaking
   Shall leap with gladness and live again.
Over the woe of the world appalling,
   Wild and sweet as a bugle cry,
Sudden I hear a new voice calling —
   "Beauty is nigh!"

Beauty is nigh!   Let the world believe it.
　Love has covered the fields of dead.
Healing is here!   Let the earth receive it,
　Greeting the Dawn with lifted head.
I sing the song of the sin forgiven,
　The deed forgotten, the wrong undone.
Lo, in the East, where the dark is riven,
　Shines the rim of the rising sun.

Healing is here!   O brother, sing it!
　Laugh, O heart, that has grieved so long.
Love will gather your woe and fling it
　Over the world in waves of song.
Hearken, mothers, and hear them coming —
　Heralds crying the day at hand.
Faint and far as the sound of drumming,
　Hear their summons across the land.

Look, O fathers!   Your eyes were holden —
　Armies throng where the dead have lain.
Fiery steeds and chariots golden —
　Gone is the dream of soldiers slain.
Sing, oh, sing of a new world waking,
　Sing of creation just begun.
Glad is the earth when morn is breaking —
　Man is facing the rising sun!

Angela Morgan

SONG OF THE UNIVERSAL

And thou, America,
For the scheme's culmination,
Its thought and its reality,
For these (not for thyself)

Thou hast arrived.
Thou, too, surroundest all,
Embracing, carrying, welcoming all;
Thou, too, by pathways broad and new
To the ideal tendest,
The measured faith of other lands,
The grandeur of the past,
Are not for thee.
But grandeurs of thine own,
Deific faiths and amplitude, absorbing,
Comprehending all,
All eligible to all.

Walt Whitman

WHAT CONSTITUTES A STATE

What constitutes a State?
Not high-raised battlement or labored mound,
    Thick wall, or moated gate;
Not cities proud with spires and turrets crowned;
    Not bays and broad-armed ports
Where, laughing at the storm, rich navies ride;
    Not starred and spangled courts,
Where low-browed baseness wafts perfume to pride;
    No! — *men!* High-minded men.

. . . . .

Men who their duties know,
But know their rights, and knowing, dare maintain,
    Prevent the long-aimed blow,
And crush the tyrant while they rend the chain:
    These constitute a State.

Sir William Jones

THE NEW STATE

O dark and cruel State
Whose towers are altars unto self alone —
   Whose streets with tears are wet,
And half thy councils given unto hate!
Shall Time not hurl thy temples stone from stone,
   And o'er the ruin set
A fairer city than the years have known?
Out of thy darkness do we find us dreams,
   And on the future gleams
The vision of thy ramparts built anew.
Mammon and War sit now a double throne,
Yet what we dream, a wiser Age shall do.

Be ye lift up, O everlasting gates
Of that far city men shall build for man!
   O fairer Day that waits,
The splendor of whose dawn we shall not see,
When selfish bonds of family and clan
Melt in the higher love that yet shall be!
O State without a master or a slave,
   Whose law of light we crave
Ere morning widen on a world set free!

George Sterling

From " Ode on the Exposition "

REDEMPTION

Loving man, I have wearied of the ways of men:
They have shut themselves up within strong walls of
   self,
The rich from the poor, the poor from the rich.
They have given themselves over to the pursuit of gold,

JUSTICE

▲

The rich and the poor.
They have lost their desire for high things;
Knowledge and wisdom and human sympathy
Have lost their ministrants. Greed and lust and pride
Have set up altars in the market-places and the homes,
And gossiping crowds throng them.

Blow, O fresh winds of God, blow through our prairie
　　lands,
Dotted with towns and villages;
Sweep, mighty tempests, through our wide city deserts;
Let the blasts from the river-cleansed Rockies
Sweep eastward to our white halls of state,
Where giant Greed has builded her shrine,
Where laws are made for a few.
Flaming fires of war, smoldering fires of peace,
Burn, burn from the heart of our life
The decay of death. Let there come forth
From the furnace of flames
A nation, God-loving, God-inspired, God-led,
Purified, transformed — a redeemed people.

Thomas Curtis Clark

AMERICA THE BEAUTIFUL

O beautiful for spacious skies,
　　For amber waves of grain,
For purple mountain majesties
　　Above the fruited plain!
　　　America! America!
　　God shed His grace on thee
And crown thy good with brotherhood
　　From sea to shining sea!

[217]

O beautiful for pilgrim feet,
Whose stern, impassioned stress
A thoroughfare for freedom beat
Across the wilderness!
America! America!
God mend thine every flaw,
Confirm thy soul in self-control,
Thy liberty in law!

O beautiful for heroes proved
In liberating strife,
Who more than self their country loved,
And mercy more than life!
America! America!
May God thy gold refine,
Till all success be nobleness,
And every gain divine!

O beautiful for patriot dream
That sees beyond the years
Thine alabaster cities gleam
Undimmed by human tears!
America! America!
God shed His grace on thee
And crown thy good with brotherhood
From sea to shining sea!

Katharine Lee Bates

On the Building of Springfield

Let not our town be large, remembering
That little Athens was the Muses' home,
That Oxford rules the heart of London still,
That Florence gave the Renaissance to Rome.

JUSTICE

Record it for the grandson of your son —
A city is not builded in a day:
Our little town cannot complete her soul
Till countless generations pass away.

Now let each child be joined as to a church
To her perpetual hopes, each man ordained:
Let every street be made a reverent aisle
Where Music grows and Beauty is unchained.

Let Science and Machinery and Trade
Be slaves of her, and make her all in all,
Building against our blatant, restless time
An unseen, skilful, medieval wall.

Let every citizen be rich toward God.
Let Christ, the beggar, teach divinity.
Let no man rule who holds his money dear.
Let this, our city, be our luxury.

We should build parks that students from afar
Would choose to starve in, rather than go home,
Fair little squares, with Phidian ornament,
Food for the spirit, milk and honeycomb.

Songs shall be sung by us in that good day,
Songs we have written, blood within the rhyme
Beating, as when Old England still was glad —
The purple, rich, Elizabethan time.

. . . . .

Say, is my prophecy too fair and far?
I only know, unless her faith be high,
The soul of this, our Nineveh, is doomed,
Our little Babylon will surely die.

JUSTICE

Some city on the breast of Illinois
No wiser and no better at the start
By faith shall rise redeemed, by faith shall rise
Bearing the western glory in her heart.

The genius of the Maple, Elm and Oak,
The secret hidden in each grain of corn,
The glory that the prairie angels sing
At night when sons of Life and Love are born,

Born but to struggle, squalid and alone,
Broken and wandering in their early years;
When will they make our dusty streets their goal,
Within our attics hide their sacred tears?

When will they start our vulgar blood athrill
With living language, words that set us free?
When will they make a path of beauty clear
Between our riches and our liberty?

We must have many Lincoln-hearted men —
A city is not builded in a day —
And they must do their work, and come and go
While countless generations pass away.

Vachel Lindsay

MY TOWN IS A CATHEDRAL

The walks are its aisles,
The trees are its pillars,
Their branches arches and ribs.

The homes are family pews,
The gardens altar flowers,
The sunsets colored glass.

[220]

JUSTICE

The lights in good men's eyes
Are living candle-flames,
Their cheery words are hymns.

Their dreams of better things
Are incense and prayers.
My town is a cathedral.

Edgar Frank

"We Builders of Cities"

We builders of cities and civilizations walled away from
the sea and the sod
Must reach, dream-led, for our revelations through one
another — as far as God.
Through one another, through one another, no more the
gleam on sea and land,
But so close that we see the Brother, and understand, and
understand!
Till, drawn in swept crowd closer, closer, we see the
gleam in the human clod,
And clerk and foreman, peddler and grocer are one in
the Family of God.

James Oppenheim

The Greatest City

What do you think endures?
Do you think the greatest city endures?
Or a teeming manufacturing state? or a prepared con-
stitution? or the best built steamships?
Or hotels of granite and iron? or any chef-d'oeuvres of
engineering, forts, armaments?

Away!   These are not to be cherished for themselves,
They fill their hour, the dancers dance, the musicians
    play for them,
The show passes, all does well enough of course,
All does very well till one flash of defiance.

The greatest city is that which has the greatest men or
    women,
If it be a few ragged huts, it is still the greatest city in
    the whole world.

Walt Whitman

From " Chants Democratic "

OVER THE GREAT CITY

Over the great city
Where the wind rustles through the parks and gardens
In the air, the high clouds brooding,
In the lines of street perspective, the lamps, the traffic,
The pavements and the innumerable feet upon them,
I Am: make no mistake — do not be deluded.

Think not because I do not appear at the first glance —
Because the centuries have gone by
And there is no assured tidings of me —
That therefore I am not there.
Think not because all goes its own way
That therefore I do not go my own way through all.
The fixed bent of hurrying faces in the street —
Each turned towards its own light, seeing no other —
Yet I am the Light towards which they all look.
The toil of so many hands to such multifarious ends,
Yet my hand knows the touch and twining of them all.

All come to me at last.
There is no love like mine;
For all other love takes one and not another;
And other love is pain, but this is joy eternal.

Edward Carpenter

VISION

The flames of God are in the streets,
The altars of truth have been set up in the market-places,
And the sons of men have become the children of God,
And have brought their sacrifices, honest hearts and
reverent spirits, to the altars.

The altars of truth have been set up in the market-places,
And the sons of men have become the children of God.
They stand with open faces in the streets, before the
altars of truth:
Their faces are uncovered, for they are not ashamed of
what they have done to other children of God.

The flames of God are in the streets,
The altars of truth have been set up in the market-places.

Thomas Curtis Clark

THE CITY'S CROWN

What makes a city great? Huge piles of stone
Heaped heavenward? Vast multitudes who dwell
Within wide circling walls? Palace and throne
And riches past the count of man to tell,
And wide domain? Nay, these the empty husk!
True glory dwells where glorious deeds are done,
Where great men rise whose names athwart the dusk

[223]

Of misty centuries gleam like the sun!
In Athens, Sparta, Florence, 'twas the soul
That was the city's bright immortal part,
The splendor of the spirit was their goal,
Their jewel the unconquerable heart!
So may the city that I love be great
Till every stone shall be articulate.

William Dudley Foulke

WHERE CROSS THE CROWDED WAYS OF LIFE

Where cross the crowded ways of life,
    Where sound the cries of race and clan,
Above the noise of selfish strife,
    We hear Thy voice, O Son of man!

In haunts of wretchedness and need,
    On shadowed thresholds dark with fears,
From paths where hide the lures of greed,
    We catch the vision of Thy tears.

From tender childhood's helplessness,
    From woman's grief, man's burdened toil,
From famished souls, from sorrow's stress,
    Thy heart has never known recoil.

The cup of water given for Thee
    Still holds the freshness of Thy grace;
Yet long these multitudes to see
    The sweet compassion of Thy face.

O Master, from the mountain side,
    Make haste to heal these hearts of pain;
Among these restless throngs abide,
    Oh tread the city's streets again.

Till sons of men shall learn Thy love,
  And follow where Thy feet have trod;
Till glorious from Thy heaven above,
  Shall come the City of our God.

Frank Mason North

THE CITY OF THE LIGHT

Hail the glorious Golden City,
  Pictured by the seers of old!
Everlasting light shines o'er it,
  Wondrous tales of love are told:
Only righteous men and women
  Dwell within its gleaming wall;
Wrong is banished from its borders,
  Justice reigns supreme o'er all.

We are builders of that City;
  All our joys and all our groans
Help to rear its shining ramparts;
  All our lives are building stones:
Whether humble or exalted,
  All are called to task divine;
All must aid alike to carry
  Forward one sublime design.

And the work that we have builded,
  Oft with bleeding hands and tears,
And in error and in anguish,
  Will not perish with our years:
It will last and shine transfigured
  In the final reign of Right;
It will merge into the splendors
  Of the City of the Light.

Felix Adler

[225]

PIONEERS

As mountain peaks that tower above the plain,
With solitude their only diadem;
Or oaks made strong in blinding storms and rain,
That ivy may the better cling to them;
As rivers flowing seaward never lag
In quest of goal, with swiftly rushing might;
Or eagles nesting on the mountain crag
Waiting, unweary, through the lonely night —
So the intrepid ones of earth, apart,
Unfriended, blaze our paths and write our creeds.

O God of Lonely Ones, fling wide your heart
And grant sufficiency to meet their needs!
Sustain — forgiving where they may have erred —
The Pioneers, who run not with the herd.

Gertrude B. Gunderson

THE NEW PATRIOT

Who is the patriot? he who lights
    The torch of war from hill to hill?
Or he who kindles on the heights
    The beacon of a world's good will?

Who is the patriot? he who sends
    A boastful challenge o'er the sea?
Or he who sows the earth with friends,
    And reaps world-wide fraternity?

Who is the patriot? It is he
    Who knows no boundary, race, or creed,
Whose nation is humanity,
    Whose countrymen all souls that need;

[226]

▲

Whose first allegiance is vowed
  To the fair land that gave him birth,
Yet serves among the doubting crowd
  The broader interests of the earth.

The soil that bred the pioneers
  He loves and guards, yet loves the more
That larger land without frontiers,
  Those wider seas without a shore.

Who is the patriot? Only he
  Whose business is the general good,
Whose keenest sword is sympathy,
  Whose dearest flag is brotherhood.

Frederic Lawrence Knowles

THE INTERNATIONALIST

Though rains of jeering pelt with hissing sneers;
  Though winds of creeds their raucous bluster shout;
Though storms of sects and parties drench the land;
  Though gales of a derision howl about;

He stands in windy storming — stands alone,
  Whom sullen raining cannot pierce or soak;
For rooted in his faith, he calmly dons
  This darkened tempest like a warming cloak.

His brow is plowed by bitterness of men,
  But scourges turn to tongues of glory yet!
His back is bent with folly of the world,
  Who takes his lashing for an epaulet!

Not all the anguish nor the bitter tears
  Can challenge Time as when his thought is heard;

[227]

Not all the thundering of all the guns
  Reverberates through ages as his word.

Banners of vision burn about his word;
  Destinies crowd and bow before his plan;
And Dawn, that kindles in his eyes, illumes
  The rising temple in the heart of man!

Louis Ginsberg

In Such an Age!

To be alive in such an age!
With every year a lightning page
Turned in the world's great wonder-book
Whereon the leaning nations look;
Where men speak strong for brotherhood
For peace and universal good;
When miracles are everywhere
And every inch of common air
Throbs a tremendous prophecy
Of greater marvels yet to be.
O Thrilling Age!
O Willing Age!
When steel and stone and rail and rod
Welcome the utterance of God
A trump to shout his wonder through
Proclaiming all that man can do.

To be alive in such an age!
To live in it!
To give in it!
Rise, soul, from thy despairing knees,
What if thy lips have drunk the lees?
The passion of a larger claim
Will put thy puny grief to shame.

JUSTICE

Fling forth thy sorrow to the wind
And link thy hope with humankind:
Breathe the world-thought, do the world-deed,
Think highly of thy brother's need.
Give thanks with all thy flaming heart,
Crave but to have in it a part —
Give thanks and clasp thy heritage —
To be alive in such an age!

Angela Morgan

THE CALL OF BROTHERHOOD

Have you heard it, the dominant call
Of the city's great cry, and the thrall
And the throb and the pulse of its life,
And the touch and the stir of its strife,
As, amid the dread dust and the din
It wages its battle of sin?
Have you felt in the crowds of the street
The echo of mutinous feet
As they march to their final release,
As they struggle and strive without peace?
Marching why, marching where, and to what!
Oh! by all that there is, or is not,
We must march too and shoulder to shoulder.
If a frail sister slip, we must hold her,
If a brother be lost in the strain
Of the infinite pitfalls of pain,
We must love him and lift him again.
For we are the Guarded, the Shielded,
And yet we have wavered and yielded
To the sins that we could not resist.
By the right of the joys we have missed,

[229]

By the right of the deeds left undone,
By the right of our victories won,
Perchance we their burdens may bear
As brothers, with right to our share.
The baby who pulls at the breast
With its pitiful purpose to wrest
The milk that has dried in the vein,
That is sapped by life's fever and drain —
The turbulent prisoners of toil,
Whose faces are black with the soil
And scarred with the sins of the soul,
Who are paying the terrible toll
Of the way they have chosen to tread,
As they march on in truculent dread —
And the Old, and the Weary, who fall —
Oh! let us be one with them all!
By the infinite fear of our fears,
By the passionate pain of our tears,
Let us hold out our impotent hands,
Made strong by Jehovah's commands,
The God of the militant poor,
Who are stronger than we to endure,
Let us march in the front of the van
Of the Brotherhood valiant of Man!

Corinne Roosevelt Robinson

OVER ALL THE LANDS

Over the prairies and over the mountains,
  And up from the cities that front the sea,
Out from the mills and the mines and the forests
  Is surging the call that shall set men free:

JUSTICE

Refrain:

Over all the lands it sounds
  And over all the waters:
" Earth and the fruits of earth
  For all earth's sons and daughters!
No more each for each alone,
  But undivided,
  With hearts decided
We rise to claim our own! "

No more shall one man grow rich from another,
  Or greed of the few thwart the common good;
Children are we of the one Mighty Mother,
  As wide as the earth in our brotherhood.

Brothers shall build us the homes that we dwell in,
  And brothers shall till for our food and soil;
Brothers in freedom shall meet with each other,
  With gladness exchanging the fruits of toil.

Brothers shall sit in the council of peoples
  With old hates forgotten and war flags furled;
Brothers shall build us the ships and the railroads
  That bind us together across the world!

Anna Louise Strong

THE FATHERLAND

Where is the true man's fatherland?
  Is it where he by chance is born?
  Doth not the yearning spirit scorn
In such scant borders to be spanned?
Oh, yes! his fatherland must be
As the blue heavens, wide and free!

[231]

Is it alone where freedom is?
  Where God is God and man is man?
  Doth he not claim a broader span
For the soul's love of home than this?
Oh, yes! his fatherland must be
As the blue heavens, wide and free!

Where'er a human heart doth wear
  Joy's myrtle-wreath or sorrow's gyves,
  Where'er a human spirit strives
After a life more true and fair,
There is the true man's birthplace grand,
His is a worldwide fatherland!

James Russell Lowell

PRAYER FOR THE TIMES

Redeemer of nations, burster of prison gates;
Lifter from broken hearts of chains and weights;
Feeder of famished hearts, joiner of hands,
Returner of exiles from alien strands;
Bringer of morning, bringer of air,
Kindler of laughter in ashes of despair!

. . . . .

Thy freemen, victorious,
Jubilantly run to Thee!
Not with shouting and singing,
Exultant trumpet or drum,
But with hearts like church bells ringing,
Conqueror, we come!
Devouring fire, invincible light!
Builder of dawn on the ruins of night!
Builder with music of the crystal halls of day,
God, we are Thine! Command and we obey!

Herman Hagedorn

The Golden Age

The golden age is in my heart today: it has cut loose
     from all the yesterdays and tomorrows and allied
     itself with today;
It has come out of the poems and pictures and prophecies,
     and fixed itself in me;
The golden age, which you have always looked back
     somewhere to see:
The golden age, which you have always looked forward
     somewhere to see:
The always postponed, defeated vision, retreating with
     your retreat, advancing with your advance:
The lure of the young, the mockery of the old, the folly
     of noontime:
The sacred, perfect world everywhere, the radiant
     flawless sundreams drawing us all, body and spirit,
     into its fairy tangle;
For the golden age is not what you take it for in time,
     but what it comes to in your heart.

Horace Traubel

The Symphony

With instruments in ill-accord a hundred men
Thrum strings that hold sweet harmonies in leash;
Twisting the keys till practiced ears are satisfied:
    And then, enticingly, in cadences that surge
    And flow like billows on a granite shore,
    The genius of a Wagner casts a lingering spell.

These are not kinsmen, save as all mankind are kin;
Of birth and tongues diverse; of customs, creeds
And laws; of dear traditions. Bound by a single tie:

And yet, entrancingly, in diapasons grand
That first invite, then move, and then enthrall,
The soul of some great master weaves a subtle spell.

The shadows of the crosses lie upon the fields.
The chastened peoples now have tuned again
Their instruments of peace. Waiting they thrum the
    strings:
Now may there swell the strains majestic of a vast
Symphony of will, sounding the war-lords' knell,
As gently weaves the Master Soul his mystic spell.

Herman W. Stillman

WHY I AM A LIBERAL

" Why? " — Because all I haply can and do,
All that I am now, all I hope to be —
Whence comes it save from fortune setting free
Body and soul, the purpose to pursue
God traced for both?   If fetters not a few,
Of prejudice, convention, fall from me,
These shall I bid men — each in his degree
Also God-guided — bear, and gaily, too?

But little do or can the best of us:
That little is achieved through Liberty.
Who, then, dares hold, emancipated thus,
His fellow shall continued bound?   Not I,
Who live, love, labor freely, nor discuss
A brother's right to freedom. — That is " Why."

Robert Browning

From MAKE OF MAN THE STATUE

Make of man the statue, the priceless piece of art.
All that Greece has given,
All that time has striven
For ages to impart,
Weld it in his sinews, mold it in his thought,
Till the humblest scavenger is gloriously wrought.
Shame upon the galleries, filled with treasures fine
While the work of Heaven, Man, who is Divine,
Shivers in the hallway, shuffles through the street,
Shambles down the alley, with weak and ragged feet.

. . . . .

Make of man the statue, make of man the building.
What avails the gilding
Of altar or of dome,
What the gorgeous tapestries blooming in the home,
What avails the splendor where stately mansions stand
If men who make the mansions are homeless in the land?
Shame upon the church spires climbing to the sky,
While the trudging millions suffer, starve and die!

. . . . .

Make of man the poem, make of man the theme,
Fruiting of the vision, flowering of the dream.
All that Rome has given,
All that Art has striven
For centuries to say,
Breathe it in his spirit, coin it in his heart,
Till the poorest laborer can share the loveliest part.
Make of man the shining, pure and perfect thing;
Give him room to grow in;
Give him fields to sow in,
Teach his lips to sing.

Shame upon the white streets, brilliant with display,
While the hungry people struggle on their way.

Make of man the towering, the beautiful emprise,
Great as any temple that reaches to the skies.
Take your " worthless derelict, ignorant and vile,"
Give him skies to dream in,
Love a chance to gleam in,
Teach his soul to smile.
Give his toil its payment,
Clothe him sweet with raiment,
Give him food to nourish,
Help his thought to flourish;
Proudly lift his head then,
Freely let him stand. . . .
All the rest is said then:
Clasp his godly hand!

Angela Morgan

THE MILLENNIUM

Ask for no mild millennium:
Our world shall never be nobler than its inhabitants:
Never be nobler than you and I, blind brother.

What is this world but our secret natures opened and
    stamped into cities?
The smoke of the mills is only the vapor of our soft-coal
    hearts:
The slums of the poor and the drab palaces of the rich
    are the filth of our spirits:
The curses of the world are but the unleashed beast in
    us roaming the streets.

▲

Here and there is one shining among us:
He is not a conqueror of tools, but a conqueror of self:
He strides like a sun in the crowds, and people are glad
    of him:
He did not wait for a millennium to perfect him:
He did not see the need of sanitation and pure food to
    help him to a soul:
He wrestled with the antagonist in his own breast and
    emerged victorious.

Give us a hundred million such, and a greater world is
    upon us:
But give us only a perfect world, and it shall be a coat
    that misfits us.
Stagnation and sin shall be there as surely as they are
    deep in our hearts.

James Oppenheim

They Who Tread the Path of Labor

They who tread the path of labor follow where My feet
    have trod;
They who work without complaining, do the holy will
    of God;
Nevermore thou needest seek me; I am with thee every-
    where;
Raise the stone, and thou shalt find Me, cleave the wood
    and I am there.

Where the many toil together, there am I among My
    own;
Where the tired workman sleepeth, there am I with him
    alone:

I, the Peace that passeth knowledge, dwell amid the daily
    strife;
I, the Bread of Heav'n am broken in the sacrament of
    life.

Every task, however simple, sets the soul that does it free;
Every deed of love and mercy, done to man is done to
    Me.
Nevermore thou needest seek me; I am with thee every-
    where;
Raise the stone, and thou shalt find Me; cleave the wood,
    and I am there.

Henry van Dyke

BEING WALKERS WITH THE DAWN

Being walkers with the dawn and morning
Walkers with the sun and morning,
We are not afraid of night,
Nor days of gloom,
Nor darkness,
Being walkers with the sun and morning.

Langston Hughes

SHE WHO IS TO COME

A woman — in so far as she beholdeth
    Her one Beloved's face;
A mother — with a great heart that enfoldeth
    The children of the Race;
A body, free and strong, with that high beauty
    That comes of perfect use, is built thereof;

JUSTICE

A mind where Reason ruleth over Duty,
    And Justice reigns with Love;
A self-poised, royal soul, brave, wise, and tender,
    No longer blind and dumb;
A Human Being, of an unknown splendor,
    Is she who is to come!

Charlotte Perkins Gilman

UNFETTERED

Written in prison

They placed him in a prison cell and put on him a
    prison suit.
God gave him Dreams, so it befell he rose from mire
    that clogs the brute.
They pigeon-holed and numbered him, but he kept faith
    and held a goal,
And stars and flowers in evening's dim conversed with
    his unfettered soul.

John Francis Glynn

MARTYRDOM

The earth cries loud for blood; for never grew
One saving truth amid the human stress,
That withered not in barren loneliness
Till watered by the sacrificial dew.
Red are the prophets: see how Athens slew
Her mortal sage for his immortal guess:
A thousand Golgothas to God confess
The cross, the crypt and, oh, the crimson hue!

Through cloud and whirlwind, agony and flame,
Man goes to God, a glory round his head:

[239]

Some one must bleed or else the world will die!
O ye who dare the shadow and the shame,
Red is the road to freedom. With our dead,
We build the steps of life into the sky!

Leonard Van Noppen

To Dreamers Everywhere

And if your own and time alike betray you,
If all you hoped and wrought for does not come,
Why should that dismay you?
Why should creeping doubt benumb
The leaping pulses of your will?
Have patience and be strong.
Seems your waiting long?
One has waited longer, who is waiting still.

Amelia Josephine Burr

No Armistice in Love's War

What are poets?   Are they only drums commanding?
Trumpets snarling, moving men to hate and ravage?
Were their songs of war the snares of Trade demanding
Lives, and binding men to gods senile and savage?

What are soldiers?   Only powers, to be broken
On the wheel of Business when there is no battle?
" War to end all war," was that but falsely spoken?
Whom has war set free?   Have rifles stopped their
    rattle?

Many suffer hunger while the few still plunder.
Dreams of peace and brotherhood are all undone.

[240]

Let poets' songs boom loud with love's own battle
thunder!
War has ended? No, the war has just begun.

Ralph Cheyney

PUBLIC SERVANT OF THE GODS

I am primarily engaged to myself,
to be a public servant of all the gods;
to demonstrate to all men
that there is intelligence
and good will at the heart of things,
and higher and yet higher leadings —
These are my engagements.
If there be power in good intentions,
in fidelity, and in toil,
the north wind shall be purer,
and the stars in heaven will glow
with a kindlier beam that I have lived.

Ralph Waldo Emerson

LOVE, GIVE ME THE FEEL OF TOMORROW

Come, love, help me move all the mirrors out of my
workshop,
All the sore spots out of my heart!
You only can give me what I need;
A steel girder faith to build on,
The feel of tomorrow in my land.
Andante of a happy city's hundred thousand feet,
Keeping step in a grand procession,
Telling the world they walk in peace and freedom,
Broadcasting a forever and ever armistice day.

Ralph Cheyney

A Loftier Race

These things shall be! a loftier race
    Than ere the world hath known shall rise
With flame of freedom in their souls,
    And light of knowledge in their eyes.

They shall be gentle, brave, and strong
    To spill no drop of blood, but dare
All that may plant man's lordship firm
    On earth, and fire, and sea, and air.

Nation with nation, land with land,
    Unarmed shall live as comrades free:
In every heart and brain shall throb
    The pulse of one fraternity.

New arts shall bloom of loftier mold
    And mightier music fill the skies,
And every life shall be a song,
    When all the earth is paradise.

John Addington Symonds

Brotherhood

O Brother man! fold to thy heart thy brother;
Where pity dwells, the peace of God is there;
To worship rightly is to love each other,
Each smile a hymn, each kindly deed a prayer.

Follow with reverent steps the great example
Of Him whose holy work was " doing good ";
So shall the wide earth seem our Father's temple,
Each loving life a psalm of gratitude.

[242]

Then shall all shackles fall; the stormy clangor
Of wild war music o'er the earth shall cease;
Love shall tread out the baleful fire of anger,
And in its ashes plant the tree of peace!

John Greenleaf Whittier

THE GREATEST OF THESE

A Paraphrase of I Corinthians, XIII

If I create wealth beyond the dream of past ages and increase not love, my heat is the flush of fever and my success will deal death.

Though I have foresight to locate the fountains of riches, and power to pre-empt them, and skill to tap them, and have no loving vision for humanity, I am blind.

Though I give of my profits to the poor and make princely endowments for those who toil for me, if I have no human fellowship of love with them, my life is barren and doomed.

Love is just and kind. Love is not greedy and covetous. Love exploits no one; it takes no unearned gain; it gives more than it gets. Love does not break down the lives of others to make wealth for itself; it makes wealth to build the life of all. Love seeks solidarity; it tolerates no divisions; it prefers equal work-mates; it shares its efficiency. Love enriches all men, educates all men, gladdens all men.

The values created by love never fail; but whether there are class privileges, they shall fail; whether there are millions gathered, they shall be scattered; and whether there are vested rights, they shall be abolished. For in the past strong men lorded it in ruthlessness and strove for their own power and

▲

pride, but when the perfect social order comes, the strong shall serve the common good. Before the sun of Christ brought in the dawn, men competed, and forced tribute from weakness, but when the full day shall come, they will work as mates in love, each for all and all for each. For now we see in the fog of selfishness, darkly, but then with social vision; now we see our fragmentary ends, but then we shall see the destinies of the race as God sees them. But now abideth honor, justice, and love; these three; and the greatest of these is love.

Walter Rauschenbusch

WORLD BROTHERHOOD

My country is the world;
My flag with stars impearled
   Fills all the skies,
All the round earth I claim,
Peoples of every name;
And all inspiring fame,
   My heart would prize.

Mine are all lands and seas,
All flowers, shrubs and trees,
   All life's design,
My heart within me thrills
For all uplifted hills,
And for all streams and rills;
   The world is mine.

And all men are my kin,
Since every man has been,
   Blood of my blood,

[244]

I glory in the grace
And strength of every race
And joy in every trace
　Of brotherhood.

The days of pack and clan
Shall yield to love of man,
　When war-flags are furled;
We shall be done with hate,
And strife of state with state,
When man with man shall mate,
　O'er all the world.

Author Unknown

O CHINA, TOWERING

O China, towering from earth to heaven,
Spreading beyond the eight horizons,
Thou Flowery Land born of the peaks,
With mighty rivers and endless ranges,
I see thee free at last, and a new era
Dawn on thy peoples for a thousand years.

Chinese National Anthem

HE WHOM A DREAM HATH POSSESSED

He whom a dream hath possessed knoweth no more of
　doubting,
For mist and the blowing of winds and the mouthing of
　words he scorns;
Not the sinuous speech of schools he hears, but a knightly
　shouting,
And never comes darkness down, yet he greeteth a
　million morns.

JUSTICE

He whom a dream hath possessed knoweth no more of
    roaming;
All roads and the flowing of waves and the speediest
    flight he knows,
But wherever his feet are set, his soul is forever homing,
And going, he comes, and coming he heareth a call and
    goes.

He whom a dream hath possessed knoweth no more of
    sorrow,
At death and the dropping of leaves and the fading of
    suns he smiles,
For a dream remembers no past, and scorns the desire
    of a morrow,
And a dream in a sea of doom sets surely the ultimate
    isles.

He whom a dream hath possessed treads the impalpable
    marches,
From the dust of the day's long road he leaps to a laugh-
    ing star,
And the ruin of worlds that fall he views from eternal
    arches,
And rides God's battlefield in a flashing and golden car.

Shaemus O'Sheel

"Till We Have Built Jerusalem"

And did those feet in ancient time
    Walk upon England's mountain green?
And was the holy Lamb of God
    On England's pleasant pastures seen?

And did the countenance divine
    Shine forth upon our clouded hills?

JUSTICE

And was Jerusalem builded here
   Among these dark Satanic mills?

Bring me my bow of burning gold!
   Bring me my arrows of desire!
Bring me my spear: O clouds, unfold!
   Bring me my chariot of fire!

I will not cease from mental fight,
   Nor shall my sword sleep in my hand,
Till we have built Jerusalem
   In England's green and pleasant land.

William Blake

From The Prophetic Book " Milton "

ODE

We are the music makers,
   And we are the dreamers of dreams,
Wandering by lone sea-breakers,
   And sitting by desolate streams —
World-losers and world-forsakers,
   On whom the pale moon gleams;
Yet we are the movers and shakers
   Of the world forever, it seems.

With wonderful deathless ditties
   We build up the world's great cities,
And out of a fabulous story
   We fashion an empire's glory:
One man with a dream, at pleasure,
   Shall go forth and conquer a crown;
And three with a new song's measure
   Can trample a kingdom down.

[247]

We, in the ages lying
  In the buried past of the earth,
Built Nineveh with our sighing,
  And Babel itself in our mirth;
And o'erthrew them with prophesying
  To the old of the new world's worth;
For each age is a dream that is dying,
  Or one that is coming to birth.

Arthur O'Shaughnessy

O Heart

O Heart, that beats with every human heart
O Heart, that weeps with every human tear,
O Heart, that sings with every human song,
Fill our slow hearts with flood-tides of Thy love;
That they may beat with every human heart,
That they may weep with every human tear,
That they may sing with every human song,
And thus, through Thee, unite with all mankind.

Maurice Rowntree

Brotherhood

The crest and crowning of all good,
  Life's final star is Brotherhood;
For it will bring again to earth
  Her long-lost Poesy and Mirth,
Will send new light on every face,
  A kingly power upon the race.
And till it comes, we men are slaves,
And travel downward to the dust of graves.

Come, clear the way then, clear the way:
Blind creeds and kings have had their day.
Break the dead branches from the path:
Our hope is in the aftermath —
Our hope is in heroic men,
Star-led to build the world again.
To this Event the ages ran:
Make way for Brotherhood — make way for Man.

Edwin Markham

GREAT IS JUSTICE!

Great is Justice!
Justice is not settled by legislators and laws — it is in
the Soul,
It cannot be varied by statutes, any more than love,
pride, the attraction of gravity, can,
It is immutable — it does not depend on majorities —
majorities or what not come at last before the same
passionless and exact tribunal.

For justice are the grand natural lawyers and perfect
judges — it is in their Souls,
It is well assorted — they have not studied for nothing
— the great includes the less,
They rule on the highest grounds — they oversee all
eras, states, administrations.

The perfect judge fears nothing — he could go front to
front before God,
Before the perfect judge all shall stand back — life and
death shall stand back — heaven and hell shall
stand back.

Walt Whitman

From " Leaves of Grass "

THE DESIRE OF NATIONS
Abridged

Earth will go back to her lost youth,
And life grow deep and wonderful as truth,
When the wise King out of the nearing heaven comes
To break the spell of long millenniums —
To build with song again
The broken hope of men —
To hush and heroize the world,
Beneath the flag of Brotherhood unfurled.
And He will come some day:
Already shines His star upon the way!
He comes, O world, He comes!
But not with bugle-cry nor roll of doubling drums.

And when He comes into the world gone wrong,
He will rebuild her beauty with a song.
To every heart He will its own dream be:
One moon has many phantoms in the sea.
Out of the North the norns will cry to men:
" Baldur the Beautiful has come again! "
The flutes of Greece will whisper from the dead:
" Apollo has unveiled his sunbright head! "
The stones of Thebes and Memphis will find voice:
" Osiris comes: O tribes of Time, rejoice! "
And social architects who build the State,
Serving the Dream at citadel and gate,
Will hail Him coming through the labor-hum.
And glad quick cries will go from man to man:
" Lo, he has come, our Christ the Artisan,
The King who loved the lilies, He has come! "

Edwin Markham

▲

The Builders

Not in the dream of yesterday is found
Substructure of the world that is to be;
The pit was digged by no lone poet's plea,
Nor did the blood of martyrs break the ground.
Fear not! they shall be well-confessed and crowned
Who played the prophets' part; yet shall men see
The work was our humanity's, and we
Are all together in the building bound.
All life was in that quickening of the hand
Which from the club wrought on to the machine;
The airy uplift of the lumbering feet
To argosies which all the heavens command;
The few as nothing, to the myriad mean
In whom man's vast adventure is complete.

Robert Whitaker

My Church

My church has but one temple,
Wide as the world is wide,
Set with a million altars,
Where a million hearts abide.

My church has no creed to bar
A single brother man,
But says, " Come thou and worship "
To every one who can.

My church has no roof nor walk
Nor floor, save the beautiful sod,
For fear I would seem to limit
The love of the illimitable God.

E. O. G.

Earth Is Enough

We men of earth have here the stuff
Of Paradise — we have enough!
We need no other stones to build
The Temple of the Unfulfilled —
No other ivory for the doors —
No other marble for the floors —
No other cedar for the beam
And dome of man's immortal dream.

   Here on the paths of every-day —
Here on the common human way —
Is all the busy gods would take
To build a heaven, to mold and make
New Edens. Ours the task sublime
To build Eternity in time!

Edwin Markham

Good News

Let me be done for good and all with news
Of a mad world, proclaimed on every side
By orators who thunder and deride,
And bitter preachers shrieking: " I accuse! "
And cynic quipsters scribbling to amuse —
Fierce wee colossi on mole-hills astride.
Where is the unreal world which they abuse?
What means the torrent of their wordy pride?

For there are folk in darkened city rooms,
Meek souls, in whom bright loving kindness blooms;
And there are folk on lonely toilsome farms,
Kind souls, who live and die without alarms;
In them th' eternal gospel speaks again,
And angels sing: Peace and good will to men.

Tertius van Dyke

"Make Tomorrow a New Morn!"

Give to barrows, trays and pans
Grace and glimmer of romance;
Bring the moonlight into noon
Hid in gleaming piles of stone;
On the city's pavèd street
Plant gardens lined with lilacs sweet;
Let spouting fountains cool the air,
Singing in the sun-baked square;
Let statue, picture, park and hall,
Ballad, flag and festival,
The past restore, the day adorn,
And make tomorrow a new morn!

. . . . .

So shall the drudge in dusty frock
Spy beside the city clock
Retinues of airy kings,
Skirts of angels, starry wings,
His fathers shining in bright fables,
His children fed at heavenly tables.

Ralph Waldo Emerson

The Ship of Democracy

Sail, sail thy best, ship of Democracy,
Of value is thy freight, 'tis not the Present only,
The Past is also stored in thee.
Thou holdest not the venture of thyself alone, not of
the Western continent alone,
Earth's resumé entire floats on thy keel, O ship, is steadied
by thy spars,
With thee Time voyages in trust, the antecedent nations
sink or swim with thee,

JUSTICE

With all their ancient struggles, martyrs, heroes, epics,
    wars, thou bearest the other continents,
Theirs, theirs as much as thine, the destination-port
    triumphant;
Steer then with good strong hand and wary eye, O
    helmsman, thou carriest great companions,
Venerable priestly Asia sails this day with thee,
And royal feudal Europe sails with thee.

Walt Whitman

From " Thou Mother With Thy Equal Brood "

SOMEWHERE ADOWN THE YEARS

Somewhere adown the years there waits a man
Who shall give wings to what my soul has said:
Shall speak for me when I am mute and dead;
And shall perfect the work I but began.

What matter, therefore, if my word today
Falls on unwilling ears, finds few to praise?
Since some mere child, in his incipient days,
That word may win to walk a prophet's way?

And he, of greater gift, more favored state,
Shall speak to thousands where I speak to one:
Shall do the work that I would fain have done;
Helped to that fortune at my lonely gate.

God will not suffer any word to fail
That is not uttered for the hour's success:
No word that has in it the power to bless
Shall lack the means to make it of avail.

Who speaks the people's weal shall some day find
Voices to bear it to the people's will.

However potent be the present ill
They who assail it are tomorrow's kind.

And that tomorrow shall uphold their cause
Who fell not for the plaudits of today:
Those who are reckoned rebels in their day
Are always makers of tomorrow's laws.

Our present skeptics voice tomorrow's faith;
Today's disturbers bring tomorrow's peace:
'Tis they who dare to die who win release
For all their fellows from the fear of death.

Robert Whitaker

LOCARNO

The half-gods go; the centaurs, too.
The tarnished halos hang askew.
The startled hoof-beats, halted, hide
Upon a cross-scarred mountain-side,
Where trampled lovers all night through
Seek brides in wreaths of maiden's rue.
These, too, shall pass.   A cooling dew
Has laid the ghosts of those who died —
    The half-gods go.

O seers, whose glow of vision blew
The haunted mists away, and you,
Unwedded elegists who cried
For gay young saviors crucified,
They rest beneath a dream come true:
    The half-gods go.

Earl Marlatt

[255]

JUSTICE

▲

A Psalm of Confidence

The spirit of Man shall triumph and reign o'er all the earth.

The earth was made for Man, he is heir to all that therein is.

He is the end of creation, the purpose of the ages since the dawn of time.

He is the fulfillment of all prophecy and is himself the goal of every great hope born in high desire.

Who art Thou, O Spirit of Man?

Thou art the Child of the Infinite, in thy nostrils is the breath of God.

Thou didst come at Love's behest, yea! to fulfill the Love of the Eternal didst Thou come.

Yet Man's beginnings were in lowliness, in nature akin to that of the brute.

His body and appetite bore the marks of the beast, yet in his soul was the unquenchable Spark of Divine Fire.

His ascending hath been with pain, with struggle and conflict hath he marched towards the Ideal.

At times he hath turned his face away from the Promise of Destiny.

He hath given reins to the lust of the brute; he hath appeared at times as the Child of Hate.

He hath forgotten his Divine Origin, he hath forsaken the dream of Eternal Love.

Then hath he lifted his hands against his fellows and war and bloodshed have dwelt upon the earth.

In moments of blind passion he hath destroyed the work of his own hands, the fruit of the centuries hath he cast to the winds.

He hath marred the Divine Image, deaf to the call of the
  Promise of God.

Upon the altars of Self hath he sacrificed Brotherhood,
  and ruled by avarice and greed he hath slain Justice
  and Right.

Thus have wickedness and sin dwelt in his midst, and his
  soul hath been chained in the bondage of low desires.

Yet all this could not destroy the unquenchable Spark
  of Divine Fire.

For it belongs to the Eternal and that which is Eternal
  cannot die.

Therefore, great though Thy shortcomings, manifold
  though Thy failures, wicked though Thy crimes;

I will not despair, O Spirit of Man!

Thou canst not forever deny the God that is within
  Thee, nor turn Thy back upon the Ideal;

Though Thou destroyest fairest hopes yet shall they live
  again.

Though Thou returnest to the level of the beast Thou
  shalt arise to the heights of Thy Divine Humanity.

For the Spirit of Man breathes the untiring purpose of
  the Living God and to the fulfillment of that purpose the whole creation moves.

Stanton Coit

From " The Spirit of Man "

You Cannot Kill the Troubadours

Though starved throughout your every city,
  Rotarian businessmen and boors,
We still defy you as we pity.
  You cannot kill the troubadours.

You blacken heaven with smokestack pencil
    And blemish nature with billboard art.
You force upon man's mind your stencil,
    But cannot quell the singing heart.

Oh, lords of factory and steeple,
    You scare the foolish, grind the poor,
Conspire against the weary people.
    You cannot daunt a troubadour.

Our song shall drown your guns and whistles,
    Inspire the meek to claim their rights.
We have forced kings to feed on thistles.
    Strong kings who fought the singer-knights.

Despised, rejected, we remember
    The land we ruled with song and amours.
The king and pope made Provence an ember
    But could not crush the troubadours.

We have swallowed our fill of " facts " and scorning.
    We have taken our stand with all the oppressed.
You will wake to our power on some red morning
    When a poem sticks like a lance in your breast.

Pollute the springs of truth and rapture.
    And rape the forests and the moors.
The singing folk elude your capture.
    You cannot kill the troubadours.

Ralph Cheyney

THE SOCIETY OF MEN

I found the Holy Spirit in the noise of cities. I found
    the Holy Spirit in the society of men. It was a gray
    mist hovering over the machines of industry. It

was a soft hand on the face of a worker there. It waited silently in the offices where the machinery of tape and paper hummed busily. It was there where men met men in the simplest and most elaborate sociabilities, the loafers in the square and the lady at her afternoon tea.

I looked for the Holy Spirit and I found it in the society of men.

Raymond Kresensky

TRUE PEACE

Drums and battle-cries
Go out in music of the morning-star —
  And soon we shall have thinkers in the place
Of fighters, each found able as a man
  To strike electric influence through a race
Unstayed by city-wall and barbican.

Elizabeth Barrett Browning

From " Casa Guidi Windows "

1914 — AND AFTER

Would you end war?
Create great Peace. . . .

.   .   .   .   .

The Peace that demands all of a man,
His love, his life, his veriest self;
Plunge him into the smelting fires of a work that becomes his child,

.   .   .   .   .

Give him a hard Peace; a Peace of discipline and justice. . . .

[259]

Kindle him with vision, invite him to joy and adventure:
Set him to work, not to create *things*
But to create *man:*
Yea, himself.

Go search your heart, America. . . .
Turn from the machine to man,
Build, while there is yet time, a creative Peace. . . .
While there is yet time! . . .
For if you reject great Peace,
As surely as vile living brings disease,
So surely will your selfishness bring war.

James Oppenheim

THE NEW DAY

Ye that have faith to look with fearless eyes
  Beyond the tragedy of a world at strife,
And know that out of death and night shall rise
  The dawn of ampler life:
Rejoice, whatever anguish rend the heart,
  That God has given you the priceless dower
To live in these great times and have your part
  In Freedom's crowning hour;
That ye might tell your sons who see the light
  High in the heavens — their heritage to take —
" I saw the powers of darkness take their flight;
  I saw the morning break! "

Owen Seaman

MARTYRS OF HUMANITY

We praise Thee, Almighty God, for Thine elect, the
  prophets and martyrs of humanity, who gave their
  thoughts and prayers and agonies for the truth of

[260]

God and the freedom of the people. We praise
Thee that amid loneliness and the contempt of men,
in poverty and imprisonment, when they were condemned by the laws of the mighty and buffeted on
the scaffold, Thou didst uphold them by Thy spirit
in loyalty to Thy holy cause.

Our hearts burn within us as we follow the bleeding feet
of Thy Christ down the centuries, and count the
mounts of anguish on which He was crucified anew
in His prophets and the true apostles of His spirit.
Help us to forgive those who did it, for some truly
thought they were serving Thee when they sup-
pressed Thy light, but oh, save us from the same
mistake!

Grant us an unerring instinct for what is right and true,
and a swift sympathy to divine those who truly
love and serve the people. Suffer us not by
thoughtless condemnation or selfish opposition to
weaken the arm and chill the spirit of those who
strive for the redemption of mankind.

May we never bring upon us the blood of all the
righteous by renewing the spirit of those who per-
secuted them in the past. Grant us rather that we,
too, may be counted in the chosen band of those
who have given their life as a ransom for the many.
Send us forth with the pathfinders of humanity
to lead Thy people another day's march toward the
land of promise.

And if we, too, must suffer loss, and drink of the bitter
pool of misunderstanding and scorn, uphold us by
Thy spirit in steadfastness and joy because we are
found worthy to share in the work and the reward
of Jesus and all the saints.

Walter Rauschenbusch

[261]

Say Not the Struggle Naught Availeth

Say not the struggle naught availeth,
  The labor and the wounds are vain,
The enemy faints not, nor faileth,
  And as things have been they remain.

If hopes were dupes, fears may be liars;
  It may be, in yon smoke concealed,
Your comrades chase e'en now the fliers,
  And, but for you, possess the field.

For while the tired waves, vainly breaking,
  Seem here no painful inch to gain,
Far back, through creeks and inlets making
  Comes silent, flooding in, the main.

And not by eastern windows only,
  When daylight comes, comes in the light;
In front, the sun climbs slow, how slowly,
  But westward, look, the land is bright.

Arthur Hugh Clough

Vision

As in a vision
I beheld the long, long trail—
Vast wilderness, with here and there a bloom
Spreading persistent grace,
That starred the arid reaches.

And all along the trail
The women passed, each with a burden;
And some bore their burden as a cross,
And staggered on, brows bent to earth,

Still unaware of guiding fire and pillared cloud of
 promise;

Others went singing!
With unsandaled feet they journeyed, singing!
And left their prints along the roughest way
For sign and signal.

And I beheld how others bore
Deep earthen jars,
Which steadfastly they filled
At every water course.
And ever thirsting lips, along the way,
They blessed with goodly drafts,
Poured from the vessels they thus carried far,
And kept all pure to serve another's need —
Crude earthen vessels, borne with such high grace
As made them precious;
Filled oftentimes at Marah's bitter springs,
With patient hopefulness
That rendered sweet the draft held out so eagerly
To assuage the thirst of those
Who journeyed steadfast on the long, long trail.

       Anne Cleveland Cheney

THE INVINCIBLE VANQUISHED

Valiant souls, recorded vanquished because their
earthly quests revealed no Grail. . . .

Though written vanquished, they will always be
The Seekers, Searchers, and Invincible;
From death they rose with holy gayety
To find the Grail, that long-sought miracle.

Theirs is a wider search now, for the heaven
Is theirs, and all the stars, and ordered ways,
And God to all such vanquished ones has given
Armor unpierceable for Questing Days!

Kathryn Wright

RING OUT, WILD BELLS

Ring out, wild bells, to the wild sky,
The flying cloud, the frosty light:
The year is dying in the night;
Ring out, wild bells, and let him die.

Ring out the old, ring in the new,
Ring, happy bells, across the snow:
The year is going, let him go;
Ring out the false, ring in the true.

Ring out the grief that saps the mind,
For those that here we see no more;
Ring out the feud of rich and poor,
Ring in redress to all mankind.

. . . . .

Ring out false pride in place and blood,
The civic slander and the spite;
Ring in the love of truth and right,
Ring in the common love of good.

Ring out old shapes of foul disease;
Ring out the narrowing lust of gold;
Ring out the thousand wars of old,
Ring in the thousand years of peace.

Ring in the valiant man and free,
The larger heart, the kindlier hand;
Ring out the darkness of the land,
Ring in the Christ that is to be.

Alfred Tennyson

THE NEW CHURCH

Churches come and go, but there has ever been but one religion.

The only religion is conscience in action.

The social conscience sees that wherever man walks there is the Holy Land.

It raises the cross of a new crusade against infidels, who deny the divine right of the people, that the will of God shall be done on earth as in heaven.

It insists that every question between men is a religious question, a question of moral economy before it becomes one of political economy.

It makes all political, industrial, and social activities the functions of a new church.

Henry Demarest Lloyd

From " Man the Social Creator "

SUDDENLY ONE DAY

*This poem was found in the pocket of an English
soldier killed in action*

Suddenly one day
The last ill shall fall away,
The last little beastliness that is in our blood

Shall drop from us as the sheath drops from the bud,
And the great spirit of man shall struggle through
And spread huge branches underneath the blue.
In any mirror, be it bright or dim,
Man will see God, staring back at him.

Author Unknown

THE MIGHTY HUNDRED YEARS
Abridged

It is the hour of man: new purposes,
  Broad-shouldered, press against the world's slow gate;
And voices from the vast eternities
  Still preach the soul's austere apostolate.

Always there will be vision for the heart,
  The press of endless passion: every goal
A traveler's tavern, whence we must depart
  On new divine adventures of the soul.

Edwin Markham

From AD PATRIAM

                      Land of my heart,
What future is before thee? Shall it be
To lie at ease, content with thy bright past,
Heedless of all the world, till idleness
Relax thy limbs, and swoln with wealth and pride
Shalt thou abandon justice and the poor?
Or shalt thou, re-awakened, scatter wide
The glorious tidings of a liberty
That lifts the latch of opportunity
First to thy children — then to all mankind?

Love of my soul — God keep thee strong and pure,
That thou shalt be a fitting messenger
To carry hope to all the sons of men.

William Dudley Foulke

The Universal Republic

Upon the skyline glows i' the dark
The Sun that now is but a spark;
    But soon will be unfurled —
The glorious banner of us all,
The flag that rises ne'er to fall,
    Republic of the World!

Victor Hugo

The Trumpeter

I blew, I blew, the trumpet loudly sounding;
I blew, I blew, the heart within me bounding;
The world was fresh and fair, yet dark with wrong,
And men stood forth to conquer at the song —
    I blew! I blew! I blew!

The field is won, the minstrels loud are crying,
And all the world is peace, and I am dying.
Yet this forgotten life was not in vain;
Enough if I alone recall the strain.
    I blew! I blew! I blew!

Thomas Wentworth Higginson

From I Served in a Great Cause

I served the great cause, the great cause served me:
There were never any debts between us, the compact
    was without obligation:
I answered its cry, it answered my cry.

[267]

JUSTICE

▲

The seed in the ground hungered for light, the light
    pierced the earth with unerring love —
We met, we ran together, appointed mates.

I served not as one who follows nor as one who leads:
I served not in abasement, on my knees, with my head
    in the dust:
I served proudly, accepted, accepting,
The cloudland phantoms never misting the prospect,
The sunshine sirens never dazing the day with their
    splendor,
Ever in my heart crowding ancient and unborn dreams,
Cresting the hills and making the valleys fertile.

I served in a great cause:
I served without heroism, without virtue, with no near
    destination of treasure.
I was on the march, I contained that which persevered
    me to ends unseen, no footsore night relaxed my
    pace.
There was only the press of invisible hands, only gray-
    brown eyes of invitation,
Only my franchised heart to fuel the fires to suns.

Horace Traubel

FULFILLING

Life will finish the work you are doing.
You are only one who has joined the workers
In the morning, at noon or toward shadows.
Countless have toiled before you,
There will be countless toiling after.

JUSTICE

▲

The crowds in the street move faster and faster,
Their eyes are on invisible clocks that speed the hours,
They move fast and faster, they must know soon. . . .

There is a cause and they are comrades. . . .

This is the word to come where men will look for truth.
On every one of the streets of all the cities
Not one of the hurrying crowds can flee this word. . . .

I say it wherever there is one anxious,
Where there is one doubting or hoping over the land,
Where prayer is, or blasphemy;
To all who cross their thresholds at evening, slowly,
To the young and enduring, the old who sit listless,
The mothers, the thinkers, the makers, the dreamers —

I write it now in ink,
The word that was written in blood —
It will come, one day, in light
For all to read.

MacKnight Black

The Ultimate Justice of the People

What constitutes the bulwark of our own liberty and
    independence?
It is not our frowning battlements, our bristling seacoast,
    our army and our navy.
Our reliance is in the love of liberty which God has
    planted in us.
Our defence is in the spirit which prizes liberty as the
    heritage of all men in all lands everywhere.
Destroy this spirit, and we have planted the seeds of
    despotism at our own doors.

▲

Those who deny freedom to others deserve it not for themselves, and, under a just God, cannot long retain it.

This country, with its institutions, belongs to the people who inhabit it.

. . . . .

Why should there not be a patient confidence in the ultimate justice of the people?

Is there any better or equal hope in the world?

Abraham Lincoln

FELLOWSHIP WITH ALL

O God, we thank Thee for this universe, our great home; for its vastness and its riches, and for the manifoldness of the life which teems upon it and of which we are part. We praise Thee for the arching sky and the blessed winds, for the driving clouds and the constellations on high. We praise Thee for the salt sea and the running water, for the everlasting hills, for the trees, and for the grass under our feet. We thank Thee for our senses by which we can see the splendor of the morning, and hear the jubilant songs of love, and smell the breath of the springtime. Grant us, we pray Thee, a heart wide open to all this joy and beauty, and save our souls from being so steeped in care or so darkened by passion that we pass heedless and unseeing when even the thornbush by the wayside is aflame with the glory of God.

Enlarge within us the sense of fellowship with all the living things, our little brothers, to whom Thou hast given this earth as their home in common with us.

We remember with shame that in the past we have exercised the high dominion of man with ruthless cruelty, so that the voice of the Earth, which should have gone up to Thee in song, has been a groan of travail. May we realize that they live, not for us alone, but for themselves and for Thee, and that they love the sweetness of life even as we, and serve Thee in their place better than we in ours.

When our use of this world is over and we make room for others, may we not leave anything ravished by our greed or spoiled by our ignorance, but may we hand on our common heritage fairer and sweeter through our use of it, undiminished in fertility and joy, that so our bodies may return in peace to the great mother who nourished them and our spirits may round the circle of a perfect life in Thee.

Walter Rauschenbusch

PIONEERS

We shall not travel by the road we make:
  Ere day by day the sound of many feet
Is heard upon the stones that now we break,
  We shall be come to where the cross-roads meet.

For us the heat by day, the cold by night,
  The inch-slow progress, and the heavy load,
And death at last to close the long grim fight
  With man and beast and stone; for them the Road.

For them the shade of trees that now we plant,
  The safe, smooth journey and the final goal,
Yea, birthright in the land of covenant —
  For us day-labor, travail of the soul.

JUSTICE

And yet the road is ours as never theirs!
   Is not one joy on us alone bestowed?
For us the Master-Joy, O Pioneers —
   We shall not travel, but we make the Road.

Author Unknown

From THE FIRES OF GOD

O blessed voices, O compassionate hands,
Calling and healing. O great-hearted brothers,
I come to you. Ring out across the lands
Your benediction, and I too will sing
With you, and haply kindle in another's
Dark desolate hour the flame you stirred in me.
O bountiful earth, in adoration meet
I bow to you; O glory of years to be,
I too will labor to your fashioning.
Go down, go down, unweariable feet,
Together we will march towards the ways
Wherein the marshaled hosts of morning wait
In sleepless watch, with banners wide unfurled
Across the skies in ceremonial state,
To greet the men who lived triumphant days,
And stormed the secret beauty of the world.

John Drinkwater

ON, SONS OF TOIL

On, sons of toil, with brain and brawn
   swing high your hammers free;
Let anvils clamor, fires relight
   the skies with majesty.

Who dareth cry romance is dead?
　who waileth for the old?
Lo, men of toil, ye crown the earth
　with radiance untold.

Uprear your towers to the clouds,
　spin ye your leagues of rails,
Forge on your mighty shapes of steel,
　fling airships to the gales.

Behold you, masters of the winds,
　lords of the lands and seas;
Before your might the nations blend,
　swept of vain boundaries.

On, ye that toil, blaze on the path
　by seers and prophets trod;
With flame of labor guide mankind,
　reveal the way to God.

Thornton Oakley

ENGLAND, ARISE!

England, arise! the long, long night is over,
　Faint in the east behold the dawn appear;
Out of your evil dream of toil and sorrow
　Arise, O England, for the day is here;
　　From your fields and hills,
　　Hark! the answer swells —
　Arise, O England, for the day is here.

By your young children's eyes so red with weeping,
　By their white faces aged with want and fear;
By the dark cities where your babes are creeping,

Naked of joy and all that makes life dear;
From each wretched slum
Let the loud cry come —
Arise, O England, for the day is here.

People of England! all your valleys call you,
High in the rising sun the lark sings clear.
Will you dream on, let shameful slumber thrall you?
Will you disown your native land so dear?
Shall it die unheard —
That sweet pleading word?
Arise, O England, for the day is here.

Forth, then, ye heroes, patriots, and lovers,
Comrades of danger, poverty, and scorn!
Mighty in faith of Freedom, your great Mother,
Giants refreshed in Joy's new-rising morn!
Come and swell the song,
Silent now so long —
England is risen! — and the day is here.

Edward Carpenter

NEW VISTAS

A day will come, in not undreamed of years,
When men shall wake with singing on their lips.
Their toil will bloom with hope, uncursed by fears;
They will not labor to the tune of whips;
They will not close their days as battered ships!
Then all shall be as gods, Olympus-born,
And joy shall grace each heart. As beauty drips
From summer dawns, so from the fields of corn
Shall gladness be shed forth on all the sons of morn.

Then lust will die, and gold will lose its lure.
No soul will gloat while others starve for bread.
The lore of love will prove the ample cure
For all earth's ills, now meetly harvested.
Each man, a king, in pride shall lift his head,
And every child, still bright with heaven's gleams,
Shall play in Eden gardens, tenanted
By fays and elves. By softly flowing streams
We men of earth shall find again our long lost dreams.

Thomas Curtis Clark

MAN-MAKING

We are all blind until we see
    That in the human plan
Nothing is worth the making if
    It does not make the man.

Why build these cities glorious
    If man unbuilded goes?
In vain we build the work, unless
    The builder also grows.

Edwin Markham

THE SUPERMAN

He will come;
I know not when, or how;
But he will walk breast-high with God, stepping among
    the stars.
Clothed in light and crowned with glory he will stride
    down the Milky Way,
Creating with a thought, building with a word.

A hundred million ages it may be until he comes, what
    does it matter?
Consider the deliberate stars — how eternity awaits their
    fulfillments.
A hundred million ages, and yet, sometimes,
Here and now, in these small primeval days — in this
    dull gloaming of creation's dawn —
Here and now, sometimes, there crackles out a tiny
    shimmering spark,
Some hint in our blind, protoplasmic lives,
Of that far, infinite torch
Whose ray shall one day touch the utmost reaches of
    space
Where life is borne.

One that has made brotherhood with the eagle and the
    hawk:
One that has made voices speak across the emptiness;
One that has laid cheer and comfort to the tired heart —
These and a thousand others are the prophecy;
These tell of the day
When the poor expedient of birth and the trouble of
    dying have been dismissed,
And all the sad advantages of the body are long forgot.
Walking as the angels walk, but greater than the angels,
He that will come will know not space or time, nor any
    limitation,
But will step across the sky, infinite, supreme, one with
    God.

Albert Bigelow Paine

From THE SINGING MAN

He sang above the vineyards of the world.
   And after him the vines with woven hands
Clambered and clung, and everywhere unfurled
   Triumphing green above the barren lands;
Till high as gardens grow, he climbed, he stood,
   Sun-crowned with life and strength, and singing toil,
And looked upon his work; and it was good;
      The corn, the wine, the oil.

He sang above the noon. The topmost cleft
   That grudged him footing on the mountain scars
He planted and despaired not; till he left
   His vines soft breathing to the host of stars.
He wrought, he tilled; and even as he sang,
   The creatures of his planting laughed to scorn
The ancient threat of deserts where there sprang
      The wine, the oil, the corn!

He sang not for abundance. — Over-lords
   Took of his tilth. Yet was there still to reap,
The portion of his labor; dear rewards
   Of sunlit day, and bread, and human sleep.
He sang for strength; for glory of the light.
   He dreamed above the furrows, " They are mine! "
When all he wrought stood fair before his sight
      With corn, and oil, and wine.

                   Josephine Preston Peabody

POEMS OF
JUSTICE

▲▲▲▲▲▲▲▲▲▲▲▲▲

INDEXES

▼

INDEX OF AUTHORS

ADLER, FELIX
The City of the Light, 225
ALCAEUS
Poverty, 40
ALLINSON, BRENT DOW
Hymn of Halsted Street, 17
AMBROSE, SAINT
How Far, O Rich, 49
ARNOLD, MATTHEW
To a Republican Friend, 152
BARKER, ELSA
The Easter Children, 96
BATES, KATHARINE LEE
America, the Beautiful, 217
BENET, LAURA
The Working Children to the
Story Teller, 98
BENTON, RITA
Our Daily Bread, 163
BIDDLE, E. K.
To a Student, 182
BLACK, MACKNIGHT
Fulfilling, 268
BLAKE, WILLIAM
London, 28
The Two Songs, 49
" Till We Have Built Jerusalem,"
246
BLUNT, HUGH FRANCIS
The Dreamer, 202
BODEN, FREDERICK C.
Out of the Coal Fields (extract),
22
BORST, RICHARD WARNER
For the New Age, 205
The Challenge of the Tillers, 103

BRALEY, BERTON
The Bread Line, 160
BRIGHT, VERNE
A Beggar in Paradise, 116
BROWN, EARL BIGELOW
Streets of Gold, 179
BROWNING, ELIZABETH BARRETT
The Bitter Cry of the Children,
88
True Peace, 259
BROWNING, ROBERT
Why I Am a Liberal, 234
BRUCE, AUBERT EDGAR
Provincialism, 158
BRYANT, WILLIAM CULLEN
Antiquity of Freedom, 67
BUCHANAN, ROBERT
The Image in the Forum, 111
The New Rome, 109
BURNET, DANA
Paper Roses, 5
Roses in the Subway, 177
BURNS, ROBERT
For A' That and A' That,
138
BURR, AMELIA J.
To Dreamers Everywhere, 240
BURTON, RICHARD
In a Sweatshop, 4
BUSHBY, D. MAITLAND
China Town, San Francisco,
22
CAINE, HALL
How Long, O Lord! 122
CANNELL, SKIPWITH
The Lean Gray Rats, 23

AUTHORS

CARLYLE, THOMAS
Two Men I Honor, 144
CARPENTER, EDWARD
England, Arise! 273
In the Deep Caves of the Heart, 196
Over the Great City, 222
CARTER, GEORGE
Ballade of Misery and Iron, 142
CHAPLIN, RALPH
Mourn Not the Dead, 184
CHENEY, ANNE C.
Vision, 262
CHENEY-NICHOLS, BETH
Realization, 178
CHEYNEY, RALPH
Comrade Jesus, 170
Love, Give Me the Feel of To-morrow, 241
No Armistice in Love's War, 240
You Cannot Kill the Trouba-dours, 257
CLARK, THOMAS CURTIS
God's Dreams, 186
Life Is a Feast, They Say, 11
New Vistas, 274
Prayer of the Poor, 99
Redemption, 216
The Touch of Human Hands, 176
Vision, 223
CLEGHORN, SARAH N.
Comrade Jesus, 172
The Golf Links Lie So Near the Mill, 96
The Incentive, 9
CLOUGH, ARTHUR HUGH
Say Not the Struggle Naught Availeth, 262
COIT, STANTON
A Nobler Order, 209

A Psalm of Confidence, 256
Sound Over All Waters, 203
CONE, HELEN GRAY
The Common Street, 173
CONFUCIUS
Pride in Poverty, 46
CORNING, HOWARD McKINLEY
Plowmen, 25
COWPER, WILLIAM
Slavery, 38
CRABBE, GEORGE
Country Life, 143
The Parish Workhouse, 59
CROSBY, ERNEST HOWARD
The Collection, 110
CULLEN, COUNTEE
Black Magdalens, 28
Simon the Cyrenian Speaks, 180
DAVIDSON, JOHN
Fleet Street Eclogues, 29
Man as God, 101
Piper, Play, 35
St. George's Day, 37
The Man Forbid, 123
DAVIES, MARY CAROLYN
The Dream-Bearer, 179
The Rulers, 183
DAWSON, MILES M.
Noblemen, 124
DEBS, EUGENE
Jesus, 48
DE LISLE, C. J. R.
The Marseillaise, 53
DRINKWATER, JOHN
The Fires of God (extract), 272
DRISCOLL, LOUISE
God's Pity, 175
E. O. G.
My Church, 251
ECCLESIASTES, BOOK OF
The Tears of the Oppressed, 136

AUTHORS

ELIOT, GEORGE
  Presentiment of Better Things
    (extract), 207
ELLIOTT, EBENEZER
  The People's Anthem, 56
EMERSON, RALPH WALDO
  A Nation's Strength, 206
  Boston Hymn (extract), 66
  Let Man Serve Law for Man,
    152
  "Make Tomorrow a New Morn,"
    253
  Public Servant of the Gods, 241
ENOCH, BOOK OF
  Palaces, 47
EURIPIDES
  Kings, 46
EVANS, FLORENCE WILKINSON
  Our Lady of Idleness, 8
  The Flower Factory, 94
  The Fugitives, 9
FALKOWSKI, E.
  Mine-Song, 164
FIELD, SARA BARD
  We Whom the Dead Have Not
    Forgiven, 128
FISHER, HELEN DWIGHT
  The Immigrant Madonna, 157
FLEXNER, HORTENSE
  Breaking the Molds, 197
FOULKE, WILLIAM DUDLEY
  Ad Patriam (extract), 266
  Justice for Womankind, 181
  The City's Crown, 223
FRANK, EDGAR
  My Town Is a Cathedral, 220
FRANK, FLORENCE KIPER
  A Girl Strike-Leader, 99
GALE, ZONA
  Children of Tomorrow, 204
  Voice, 188
  Women, 78

GATES, ROBERT
  Our Trade, 97
GIBSON, WILFRID WILSON
  Fires, 165
GILBERT, WILLIAM B.
  Profit or Loss, 113
GILDER, RICHARD WATSON
  Guardians of a Holy Trust, 108
GILMAN, CHARLOTTE PERKINS
  Child Labor, 95
  She Who Is to Come, 238
  The Wolf at the Door, 13
  To Labor, 85
GILTINAN, CAROLINE
  The Hungry, 168
GINSBERG, LOUIS
  The Internationalist, 227
GLYNN, JOHN FRANCIS
  Judge Not, 180
  Unfettered, 239
GOLDSMITH, OLIVER
  The Deserted Village (extract), 140
GRANICH, IRWIN
  The Little Children, 6
GUITERMAN, ARTHUR
  The Voice Unto Pharaoh, 130
GUNDERSON, GERTRUDE B.
  Pioneers, 226
HABAKKUK
  Wall Street, 600 B.C., 46
HAGEDORN, HERMANN
  Broadway, 4
  Fifth Avenue, 1915, 105
  Prayer for the Times, 232
HAMILTON, CHARLES GRANVILLE
  Business, 80
HARRISON, HENRY
  Pride, 183
HARRISON, KARL C.
  We Make Iron in Birmingham, 21
HARTSOCK, ERNEST
  Götterdämmerung, 120

[283]

AUTHORS

HEINE, HEINRICH
  Weavers, 39
HIGGINSON, THOMAS WENTWORTH
  Heirs of Time, 82
  The Trumpeter, 267
HILL, SYLVIA
  Prayer for Spring, 182
HOOD, THOMAS
  The Song of the Shirt, 32
HOUSMAN, A. E.
  Injustice, 129
HOWELLS, WILLIAM DEAN
  Society, 104
HUGHES, LANGSTON
  Being Walkers With the Dawn,
    238
  I, Too, 119
  The Negro, 27
  We Have Tomorrow, 119
HUGO, VICTOR
  Children of the Poor, 91
  Les Miserables (extract), 65
  The Universal Republic, 267
ISAIAH
  Good Tidings Unto the Meek, 136
  Legislators, 45
  Your Hands Are Full of Blood, 45
JAMES, EPISTLE OF
  Go to Now, Ye Rich, 47
JOB, BOOK OF
  Prosperity, 137
JOHNSON, JAMES WELDON
  To America, 118
JONES, ERNEST
  Song of the Lower Classes, 57
JONES, SIR WILLIAM
  What Constitutes a State? 215
KINGSLEY, CHARLES
  Bad Squire, 109
  People's Song, 1849, 58
KNOWLES, FREDERIC LAWRENCE
  The New Patriot, 226

KORAN, THE
  Concerning Usury, 137
KRESENSKY, RAYMOND
  At the Workers' Benches, 170
  Christ on Madison Street, 20
  The Society of Men, 258
  Voices, 174
KREYMBORG, ALFRED
  Factories, 6
LAMENNAIS, ROBERT DE
  Brotherhood, 138
LANIER, SIDNEY
  Trade, 82
LE GALLIENNE, RICHARD
  A Ballad of London, 107
LEITCH, MARY SINTON
  Before, 147
LE PRADE, RUTH
  The Lost Joy (extract), 143
LIEBERMAN, ELIAS
  Dawn After Christmas, 24
LI HUNG CHANG
  The Sad Sight of the Hungry,
    41
LINCOLN, ABRAHAM
  The Ultimate Justice of the Peo-
    ple, 269
LINDSAY, VACHEL
  On the Building of Springfield,
    218
  The Leaden-Eyed, 93
LLOYD, HENRY DEMAREST
  The New Church, 265
LOWE, ROBERT LIDDELL
  Woman Plowing, 26
LOWELL, JAMES RUSSELL
  A Parable, 145
  Freedom, 151
  The Fatherland, 231
  The Present Crisis (extract), 68
  The Vision of Sir Launfal (ex-
    tract), 153

AUTHORS

LUCAS, JUNE
  Blind, 181
MACKAY, CHARLES
  The Children's Auction, 34
MARKHAM, EDWIN
  Brotherhood, 248
  Conscripts of the Dream, 212
  Earth Is Enough, 252
  If He Should Come, 190
  Man-Making, 275
  The Desire of Nations, 250
  The Man Under the Stone, 81
  The Man With the Hoe, 69
  The Mighty Hundred Years, 266
  The Toiler, 74
MARLATT, EARL
  Locarno, 255
MASEFIELD, JOHN
  A Consecration, 135
MAUPIN, WILL M.
  A Song of Labor, 85
MAZZINI, JOSEPH
  The Spirit of Brotherhood, 195
MITCHELL, CYPRUS R.
  Faces, 23
MONROE, HARRIET
  The Shadow Child, 11
MOODY, WILLIAM VAUGHN
  Gloucester Moors (extract), 149
MORGAN, ANGELA
  In Such an Age, 228
  Make of Man the Statue (extract), 235
  Song of the New World, 213
  The Titan (extract), 77
MORRIS, LEWIS
  Brotherhood, 201
MORRIS, WILLIAM
  The Day is Coming, 199
  The March of the Workers, 62
  The Voice of Toil, 60

NEIHARDT, JOHN G.
  Cry of the People, 128
NORTH, FRANK MASON
  Where Cross the Crowded Ways of Life, 224
OAKLEY, THORNTON
  On, Sons of Toil, 272
OPPENHEIM, JAMES
  Bread and Roses, 124
  Confession, 187
  From a New York Skyscraper, 127
  1914 — and After, 259
  Pittsburgh, 15
  The Child, 178
  The Millennium, 236
  "We Builders of Cities," 221
O'REILLY, JOHN BOYLE
  In Bohemia, 112
O'SHAUGHNESSY, ARTHUR
  Ode, 247
O'SHEEL, SHAEMUS
  We Whom a Dream Hath Possessed, 245
Ō-SHI-O
  When I Think of the Hungry People, 138
PAINE, ALBERT BIGELOW
  The Superman, 275
PEABODY, JOSEPHINE PRESTON
  The Singing Man (extract), 277
PLATO
  Seeking Causes, 47
PLOTKIN, DAVID GEORGE
  Invocation, 24
PORTER, KENNETH W.
  Hammer and Nails, 167
  To a Prince of the Church, 115
POTEAT, JR., EDWIN McNEILL
  The Jericho Road, 106
POTTIER, EUGENE
  The Internationale, 55

AUTHORS

POUND, EZRA
Piccadilly, 177
RAUSCHENBUSCH, WALTER
Fellowship With All, 270
Martyrs of Humanity, 260
The Greatest of These, 243
The Innocent Ones Who Come
After, 189
RIDGE, LOLA
To the Free Children, 125
ROBINSON, CORINNE ROOSEVELT
The Call of Brotherhood, 229
ROLLAND, ROMAINE
Two Dwelling Places, 211
ROSENFELD, MORRIS
A Cry from the Ghetto, 2
ROWNTREE, MAURICE
O Heart, 248
SADI
The Groans of Wounded Souls,
137
SANDBURG, CARL
A Fence, 127
Prairie (extract), 187
Smoke and Steel (extract), 16
The Four Brothers (extract), 121
The Poor, 148
The Street Window, 21
They Will Say, 98
Work Gangs (extract), 160
SCHAUFFLER, ROBERT HAVEN
"Scum o' the Earth," 153
Trash, 159
SEAMAN, HELEN
L'Homme Machine, 16
SEAMAN, OWEN
The New Day, 260
SHELLEY, PERCY BYSSHE
Song to the Men of England, 50
The Mask of Anarchy, 52
SHILLITO, EDWARD
Priest and Levite, 116

SIGMUND, JAY G.
Christ in the Street, 171
SINCLAIR, MARY CRAIG
Laughter, 169
Seedlings, 10
To a Rich Young Man, 105
SINCLAIR, UPTON
On a Steamship, 148
The Menagerie, 102
SMITH, L. W.
Under the Tan, 157
SOUTHEY, ROBERT
Wat Tyler, 54
SPENCER, FANNY BIXBY
Renunciation, 183
The Russian Immigrant Grand-
mother, 19
SPENCER, LEE
How? 100
The Tread of the Poor, 40
STEINER, RICHARD M.
In a Two Million Dollar Chapel,
112
STERLING, GEORGE
In the Market-Place, 1
The New State, 216
STIDGER, WILLIAM L.
We are the Burden-Bearers,
166
STILLMAN, HERMAN W.
The Symphony, 233
STRONG, ANNA LOUISE
City Comradeship, 174
Over All the Lands, 230
SWINBURNE, ALGERNON CHARLES
A Marching Song, 64
SYMONDS, JOHN ADDINGTON
A Loftier Race, 242
TAI CHI TAO
No Resting Place, 114
TENNYSON, ALFRED
Locksley Hall (extract), 211

AUTHORS

Locksley Hall Fifty Years After (extract), 140

Ring Out, Wild Bells, 264

TOLSTOY, LEO
A Confession of Faith, 196
My Religion, 147

TOWNE, CHARLES HANSON
Manhattan, 2

TRAUBEL, HORACE
I Served in a Great Cause (extract), 267
The Golden Age, 233

TRENT, LUCIA
A White Woman Speaks, 117
Black Men, 118
Failures, 184
Prison, 26

UNDERWOOD, JOHN CURTIS
Mill Children, 5
The Weak, 87

UNTERMEYER, LOUIS
Caliban in the Coal Mines, 103

VAN DYKE, HENRY
Children of Toil, 92
They Who Tread the Path of Labor, 237

VAN DYKE, TERTIUS
Good News, 252

VAN NOPPEN, LEONARD
Martyrdom, 239

VIERECK, GEORGE S.
Nineveh (extract), 71

WADDELL, ELIZABETH
Crusaders, 114

WAGNER, RICHARD
The Revolution, 61

WHITAKER, ROBERT
Somewhere Adown the Years, 254
The Builders, 251

WHITMAN, WALT
As a Strong Bird on Pinions Free, 205
Great is Justice, 249
Pioneers! O Pioneers (extract), 193
Song of the Universal, 214
The Dear Love of Comrades, 199
The Greatest City, 221
The Ship of Democracy, 253
The Sorrows of the World, 42
They Are All for You, 185
Years of the Unperformed, 208

WHITTIER, JOHN GREENLEAF
Brotherhood, 242

WIDDEMER, MARGARET
God and the Strong Ones, 83
The Factories, 161

WILDE, OSCAR
The Ballad of Reading Gaol, 101

WILDMAN, MARION W.
On Seeing a Picture of Christ in a Junk Shop, 117

WILLIAMS, FRANCES B.
The Price of Sugar, 93
The Prop, 94

WOOD, CHARLES ERSKINE SCOTT
Sweat-Shop Slaves, 162
The Devil's Auction, 169
The Mammon Monster, 71

WORDSWORTH, WILLIAM
Written in London, September, 1802, 51

WRIGHT, KATHRYN,
The Invincible Vanquished, 263

WUPPERMAN, CARLOS
Tonight, 10

ZATURENSKY, MARYA
Song of a Factory Girl, 7

INDEX OF TITLES

Ad Patriam
  Foulke, 266
America the Beautiful
  Bates, 217
Antiquity of Freedom, The
  Bryant, 67
As a Strong Bird on Pinions Free
  Whitman, 205
At the Workers' Benches
  Kresensky, 170
Bad Squire (extract)
  Kingsley, 109
Ballad of London, A
  Le Gallienne, 107
Ballad of Reading Gaol, The (extract)
  Wilde, 101
Ballade of Misery and Iron
  Carter, 142
Battle Hymn of the Chinese Revolution, 120
Before
  Leitch, 147
Beggar in Paradise, A
  Bright, 116
Being Walkers With the Dawn
  Hughes, 238
Bitter Cry of the Children, The
  Browning, 88
Black Magdalens
  Cullen, 28
Black Men
  Trent, 118
Blind
  Lucas, 181

Boston Hymn
  Emerson, 66
Bread and Roses
  Oppenheim, 124
Bread Line, The
  Braley, 160
Breaking the Molds
  Flexner, 197
Broadway
  Hagedorn, 4
Brotherhood
  Lamennais, 138
Brotherhood
  Markham, 248
Brotherhood
  Morris, 201
Brotherhood
  Whittier, 242
Builders, The
  Whitaker, 251
Business
  Hamilton, 80
Caliban in the Coal Mines
  Untermeyer, 103
Call of Brotherhood, The
  Robinson, 229
Challenge of the Tillers, The
  Borst, 103
Cheated Child, The
  Author Unknown, 97
Child, The
  Oppenheim, 178
Child Labor
  Gilman, 95

TITLES

Children of the Poor, The
  Hugo, 91
Children of Toil
  van Dyke, 92
Children of Tomorrow
  Gale, 204
Children's Auction, The
  Mackay, 34
China Town, San Francisco
  Bushby, 22
Christ in the Street
  Sigmund, 171
Christ on Madison Street
  Kresensky, 20
City Comradeship
  Strong, 174
City of the Light, The
  Adler, 225
City's Crown, The
  Foulke, 223
Collection, The
  Crosby, 110
Common Street, The
  Cone, 173
Comrade Jesus
  Cheyney, 170
Comrade Jesus
  Cleghorn, 172
Concerning Usury
  From the Koran, 137
Confession
  Oppenheim, 187
Confession of Faith, A
  Tolstoy, 196
Conscripts of the Dream
  Markham, 212
Consecration, A
  Masefield, 135
Country Life
  Crabbe, 143
Crusaders
  Waddell, 114

Cry from the Ghetto, A
  Rosenfeld, 2
Cry of the People
  Neihardt, 128
Dawn After Christmas
  Lieberman, 24
Day Is Coming, The
  Morris, 199
Dear Love of Comrades, The
  Whitman, 199
Deserted Village, The (extract)
  Goldsmith, 140
Desire of Nations, The
  Markham, 250
Devil's Auction, The
  Wood, 169
Dream-Bearer, The
  Davies, 179
Dreamer, The
  Blunt, 202
Earth Is Enough
  Markham, 252
Easter Children, The
  Barker, 96
England, Arise!
  Carpenter, 273
Faces
  Mitchell, 23
Factories,
  Kreymborg, 6
Factories, The
  Widdemer, 161
Failures
  Trent, 184
Fatherland, The
  Lowell, 231
Fellowship With All
  Rauschenbusch, 270
Fence, A
  Sandburg, 127
Fifth Avenue, 1915
  Hagedorn, 105

[289]

TITLES

Fires,
  Gibson, 165
Fires of God, The (extract)
  Drinkwater, 272
Fleet Street Eclogues
  Davidson, 29
Flower Factory, The
  Evans, 94
For A' That and A' That
  Burns, 138
For the New Age
  Borst, 205
Four Brothers, The (extract)
  Sandburg, 121
Freedom
  Lowell, 151
From a New York Skyscraper
  Oppenheim, 127
Fugitives, The
  Evans, 9
Fulfilling
  Black, 268
Girl Strike-Leader, A
  Frank, 99
Gloucester Moors (extract)
  Moody, 149
" Go To Now, Ye Rich "
  From the Epistle of James, 47
God and the Strong Ones
  Widdemer, 83
God of the Social Passion, The
  Author Unknown, 186
God's Dreams
  Clark, 186
God's Pity
  Driscoll, 175
Golden Age, The
  Traubel, 233
Golf Links Lie So Near the Mill
  Cleghorn, 96
Good News
  van Dyke, 252

" Good Tidings Unto the Meek "
  Isaiah, 136
Götterdämmerung
  Hartsock, 120
Great Is Justice
  Whitman, 249
Greatest City, The
  Whitman, 221
Greatest of These, The
  Rauschenbusch, 243
Groans of Wounded Souls, The
  Sadi, 137
Guardians of a Holy Trust
  Gilder, 108
Hammer and Nails
  Porter, 167
He Whom a Dream Hath Possessed
  O'Sheel, 245
Heirs of Time
  Higginson, 82
Holy Week
  Whitaker, 112
How?
  Spencer, 100
How Far, O Rich
  St. Ambrose, 49
How Long, O Lord!
  Caine, 122
Hungry, The
  Giltinan, 168
Hymn of Halsted Street
  Allinson, 17
I Am the Immigrant
  Author Unknown, 19
I Served in a Great Cause (extract)
  Traubel, 267
I, Too
  Hughes, 119
If He Should Come
  Markham, 190

TITLES

Image in the Forum, The
  Buchanan, 111

Immigrant Madonna, The
  Fisher, 157

In a Sweatshop
  Burton, 4

In a Two Million Dollar Chapel
  Steiner, 113

In Bohemia
  O'Reilly, 112

In Such an Age
  Morgan, 228

In the Deep Caves of the Heart
  Carpenter, 196

In the Market-Place
  Sterling, 1

" In the Society of Men "
  Kresensky, 258

Incentive, The
  Cleghorn, 9

Injustice
  Housman, 129

Innocent Ones Who Come After, The
  Rauschenbusch, 189

Internationale, The
  Pottier, 55

Internationalist, The
  Ginsberg, 227

Invincible Vanquished, The
  Wright, 263

Invocation
  Plotkin, 24

Jericho Road, The
  Poteat, 106

Jesus
  Debs, 48

Judge Not
  Glynn, 180

Justice for Womankind
  Foulke, 181

Kings
  Euripides, 46

Laughter
  Sinclair, 169

Leaden-Eyed, The
  Lindsay, 93

Lean Gray Rats, The
  Cannell, 23

Legislators
  Isaiah, 45

Les Miserables (extract)
  Hugo, 65

Let Man Serve Law for Man
  Emerson, 152

L'Homme Machine
  Seaman, 16

Life Is a Feast, They Say
  Clark, 11

Little Children, The
  Granich, 6

Locarno
  Marlatt, 255

Locksley Hall (extract)
  Tennyson, 211

Locksley Hall Fifty Years After (extract)
  Tennyson, 140

Loftier Race, A
  Symonds, 242

London
  Blake, 28

Lost Joy, The (extract)
  Le Prade, 143

Love, Give Me the Feel of Tomorrow
  Cheyney, 241

Make of Man the Statue (extract)
  Morgan, 235

" Make Tomorrow a New Morn! "
  Emerson, 253

Mammon Monster, The
  Wood, 71

TITLES

Man as God
  Davidson, 101
Man Forbid, The
  Davidson, 123
Manhattan
  Towne, 2
Man-Making
  Markham, 275
Man Under the Stone, The
  Markham, 81
Man With the Hoe, The
  Markham, 69
March of the Hungry Men
  Author Unknown, 73
March of the Workers, The
  Morris, 62
Marching Song, A
  Swinburne, 64
Marseillaise, The
  de Lisle, 53
Martyrdom
  Van Noppen, 239
Martyrs of Humanity
  Rauschenbusch, 260
Mask of Anarchy, The
  Shelley, 52
Menagerie, The
  Sinclair, 102
Mighty Hundred Years, The
  Markham, 266
Mill Children
  Underwood, 5
Millennium, The
  Oppenheim, 236
Mine-Song
  Falkowski, 164
Mourn Not the Dead
  Chaplin, 184
My Church
  E. O. G., 251
My Religion
  Tolstoy, 147

My Town is a Cathedral
  Frank, 220
Nation's Strength, A
  Emerson, 206
Negro, The
  Hughes, 27
New Church, The
  Lloyd, 265
New Day, The
  Seaman, 260
New Patriot, The
  Knowles, 226
New Rome, The
  Buchanan, 109
New State, The
  Sterling, 216
New Vistas
  Clark, 274
1914 — and After
  Oppenheim, 259
Nineveh (extract)
  Viereck, 71
No Armistice in Love's War
  Cheyney, 240
No Resting Place
  Tai Chi Tao, 114
Noblemen
  Dawson, 124
Nobler Order, A
  Coit, 209
O China, Towering
  (Chinese National Anthem)
  245
O Heart
  Rowntree, 248
Ode
  O'Shaughnessy, 247
On a Steamship
  Sinclair, 148
On Seeing a Picture of Christ in a
  Junk Shop
  Wildman, 117

[292]

TITLES

On, Sons of Toil
  Oakley, 272
On the Building of Springfield
  Lindsay, 218
Our Daily Bread
  Benton, 163
Our Lady of Idleness
  Evans, 8
Our Trade
  Gates, 97
Out of the Coalfields (extract)
  Boden, 22
Over All the Lands
  Strong, 230
Over the Great City
  Carpenter, 222
Palaces
  From the Book of Enoch, 47
Paper Roses
  Burnet, 5
Parable, A
  Lowell, 145
Parish Workhouse, The
  Crabbe, 59
People's Anthem, The
  Elliot, 56
People's Song, 1849
  Kingsley, 58
Piccadilly
  Pound, 177
Pioneers
  Author Unknown, 271
Pioneers
  Gunderson, 226
Pioneers! O Pioneers! (extract)
  Whitman, 193
Piper, Play!
  Davidson, 35
Pittsburgh
  Oppenheim, 15
Plowmen
  Corning, 25

Poems of West Ham (extract)
  Author Unknown, 30
Poor, The
  Sandburg, 148
Poverty
  Alcaeus, 40
Prairie (extract)
  Sandburg, 187
Prayer for Spring
  Hill, 182
Prayer for the Times
  Hagedorn, 232
Prayer of the Poor
  Clark, 99
Present Crisis, The (extract)
  Lowell, 68
Presentiment of Better Things (extract)
  Eliot, 207
Price of Sugar, The
  Williams, 93
Pride
  Harrison, 183
Pride in Poverty
  Confucius, 46
Priest and Levite
  Shillito, 116
Prison
  Trent, 26
Profit or Loss
  Gilbert, 113
Prop, The
  Williams, 94
Prosperity
  Book of Job, 137
Provincialism
  Bruce, 158
Psalm of Confidence, A
  Coit, 256
Public Servant of the Gods
  Emerson, 241

TITLES

Realization
  Cheney-Nichols, 178
Redemption
  Clark, 216
Renunciation
  Spencer, 183
Revolution, The
  Wagner, 61
Ring Out, Wild Bells
  Tennyson, 264
Roses in the Subway
  Burnet, 177
Rulers, The
  Davies, 183
Russian Immigrant Grandmother,
  The
  Spencer, 19
Sad Sight of the Hungry, The
  Li Hung Chang, 41
Say Not the Struggle Naught
  Availeth
  Clough, 262
" Scum o' the Earth "
  Schauffler, 153
Seedlings
  Sinclair, 10
Seeking Causes
  Plato, 47
Shadow Child, The
  Monroe, 11
She Who Is to Come
  Gilman, 238
Ship of Democracy, The
  Whitman, 253
Simon the Cyrenian Speaks
  Cullen, 180
Singing Man, The (extract)
  Peabody, 277
Slavery
  Cowper, 38
Smoke and Steel (extract)
  Sandburg, 16

Society
  Howells, 104
Society of Men, The
  Kresensky, 258
Somewhere Adown the Years
  Whitaker, 254
Song of a Factory Girl
  Zaturensky, 7
Song of Labor, A
  Maupin, 85
Song of the Lower Classes
  Jones, 57
Song of the New World
  Morgan, 213
Song of the Shirt, The
  Hood, 32
Song of the Universal
  Whitman, 214
Song to the Men of England
  Shelley, 50
Sorrows of the World, The
  Whitman, 42
Sound Over All Waters
  Coit, 203
Spirit of Brotherhood, The
  Mazzini, 195
St. George's Day
  Davidson, 37
Street Window, The
  Sandburg, 21
Streets of Gold
  Brown, 179
Suddenly One Day
  Author Unknown, 265
Superman, The
  Paine, 275
Surf of the Slums, The
  Author Unknown, 37
Sweat-Shop Slaves
  Wood, 162
Symphony, The
  Stillman, 233

TITLES

Tears of the Oppressed, The
  Ecclesiastes, 136
They Are All for You
  Whitman, 185
They Who Tread the Path of Labor
  van Dyke, 237
They Will Say
  Sandburg, 98
"Till We Have Built Jerusalem"
  Blake, 246
Titan, The (extract)
  Morgan, 77
To America (extract)
  Johnson, 118
To a Prince of the Church
  Porter, 115
To a Republican Friend
  Arnold, 152
To a Rich Young Man
  Sinclair, 105
To a Student
  Biddle, 182
To Dreamers Everywhere
  Burr, 240
To Labor
  Gilman, 85
To the Free Children
  Ridge, 125
Toiler, The
  Markham, 74
Tonight
  Wupperman, 10
Touch of Human Hands, The
  Clark, 176
Trade
  Lanier, 82
Trash
  Schauffler, 159
Tread of the Poor
  Spencer, 40
True Peace
  Browning, 259

Trumpeter, The
  Higginson, 267
Two Dwelling Places
  Rolland, 211
Two Men I Honor
  Carlyle, 144
Two Songs, The
  Blake, 49
Ultimate Justice of the People, The
  Lincoln, 269
Under the Tan
  Smith, 157
Universal Republic, The
  Hugo, 267
Vision
  Cheney, 262
Vision
  Clark, 223
Vision of Sir Launfal, The (extract)
  Lowell, 153
Voice
  Gale, 188
Voice of Toil, The
  Morris, 60
Voice Unto Pharaoh, The
  Guiterman, 130
Voices
  Kresensky, 174
Wall Street, 600 B.C.
  Habakkuk, 46
Wat Tyler
  Southey, 54
We Are the Burden-Bearers
  Stidger, 166
"We Builders of Cities"
  Oppenheim, 221
We Have Tomorrow
  Hughes, 119
We Make Iron in Birmingham
  Harrison, 21

We Whom the Dead Have Not
   Forgiven
   Field, 128
Weak, The
   Underwood, 87
Weavers
   Heine, 39
What Constitutes a State
   Jones, 215
"When I think of the Hungry
   People"
   Ō-Shi-O, 138
Where Cross the Crowded Ways of
   Life
   North, 224
White Woman Speaks, A
   Trent, 117
Why I Am a Liberal
   Browning, 234
Wolf at the Door, The
   Gilman, 13

Woman Plowing
   Lowe, 26
Women
   Gale, 78
Work Gangs (extract)
   Sandburg, 160
Working Children to the Story
   Teller, The
   Benét, 98
World Brotherhood
   Author Unknown, 244
Written in London, September,
   1802
   Wordsworth, 51
Years of the Unperformed
   Whitman, 208
You Cannot Kill the Troubadours
   Cheyney, 257
Your Hands Are Full of Blood
   Isaiah, 45

INDEX OF FIRST LINES

A bar of steel — it is only, 16
A day will come, 274
A god is dying, 120
A laborer in Christian England, 109
A summer under open skies, 93
A thousand starve, a few are fed, 109
A wan-cheeked girl, with faded eyes, 177
A white-faced, stubborn little thing, 99
A woman — in so far, 238
A wreck? Who gave you right, 180
Ah, London! London, our delight, 107
Ah, who are these, 92
All night, without the gates, 148
All of the boxes and cartons of glass, 80
Always the poor are with us, 40
Among the mountains I wandered, 148
And did those feet, 246
And if your own and time, 240
And the voice that was softer, 153
And thou, America, 214
Arise, ye prisoners of starvation, 55
As in a vision I beheld, 262
As mountain peaks that tower, 226
As we come marching, 124
As wrinkled as the wind-swept firth, 19
Ask for no mild millennium, 236

At the gate of the West I stand, 153
Be still, my soul, 129
Beautiful, tragical faces, 177
Beautiful World of new superber Birth, 205
Beauty never visits mining places, 22
Before I brand a brother, 147
Being walkers with the dawn, 238
Bowed by the weight of centuries, 69
Brave bastion of a faith outworn, 112
Buried in one-eyed dungeons, 6
"Christ the Lord is risen," 96
Churches come and go, 265
Come, Children of Tomorrow, 204
Come hither, lads, 199
Come, love, help me move all, 241
Doth some one say that there be gods, 46
Do ye hear the children weeping, 88
Dreams are they, 186
Drums and battle-cries, 259
Each morning, faces, faces, 23
Earth will go back, 250
England, arise! 273
Face on face in the city, 174
Forgive, dear God, that we have sought, 186
For still the new transcends, 209
For the finer spirits of the world, 211

▲

For the joy of cool, green places, 99

Freedom, one of the greatest blessings, 120

Friends, the hour in which we live, 65

From a high place I saw the city, 30

From street and square, 82

From the ominous vast of the city, 37

Give me a crown of thorns, 183

Give thanks, O heart, for the high souls, 212

Give to barrows, trays and pans, 253

"Give us this day our daily bread," 163

Go to now, ye rich men, 47

God, dear God! Does she know her port, 149

God knows it, I am with you, 152

God made a race of plowmen, 25

God pity all the brave, 175

God said, "I am tired of kings," 66

God, we don't like to complain, 103

Good-night is the word, 121

Great is Justice, 249

Guardians of a holy trust, 108

Haggard faces and trembling knees, 142

Hag-haunted men who stare, 24

Hail the glorious Golden City, 225

Have the elder races halted, 193

Have you heard it, 229

He came to earth, one blue-skied day, 171

He never spoke a word to me, 180

He sang above the vineyards, 277

He saw the noonday sun, 181

He whom a dream hath possessed, 245

He will come, 275

Hear the word of the Lord, 45

Here are the faces of women, 22

Here in the furnace City, 2

How camest thou by the roses, 5

How do they live, 100

How far, O rich, 49

How like the stars are these, 4

How vain! he cried, 101

How would you have us, as we are, 118

I am primarily engaged to myself, 241

I am the dreamless dark of the mines, 164

I am the Negro, 27

I believe in God, 196

I blew, I blew, the trumpet, 267

I cannot see the stars, 37

I cannot wax ecstatic, 112

I cry to the mountains, 128

I fear the poor, 124

I found the Holy Spirit, 258

I hail you, "Dreamers," 202

I have a suit of new clothes, 138

I have builded your towns, 85

I have shut my little sister, 161

I hear it is charged, 199

I heard an angel singing, 49

I heard men saying, 60

I hope that the streets of Heaven, 179

I judge all the Dagoes, 158

I know not whether laws be right, 101

I know the road to Jericho, 106

I looked and saw a splendid, 104

I looked for Christ on Madison Street, 20

I passed the plate in church, 110

FIRST LINES

I saw a sickly cellar plant, 9
I see a monster, 71
I see my white-faced sisters, 162
I served the great cause, 267
I sing the song of a new Dawn, 213
I sit and look out upon all the
 sorrows, 42
I, too, for light the world explore,
 29
I, too, sing America, 119
I tramped the pavement, 170
I walked today along a city street,
 117
I wander through each chartered
 street, 28
I was born into this world, 97
If I create wealth, 243
If Jesus should tramp the streets,
 190
Ill fares the land, 140
In Babylon, high Babylon, 1
In massive Gothic majesty it stands,
 113
In the deep caves of the heart, 196
In the dreams of your downy
 couches, 73
Into the woods I wandered, 178
Is it well that while we range with
 Science, 140
Is there for honest poverty, 138
It is the hour of man, 266
Italians, Magyars, aliens all, 157
It's hard to breathe in a tene-
 ment, 7
Land of my heart, 266
Let crowded city pavements, 182
Let man serve law for man, 152
Let me be done for good, 252
Let not our town be large, 218
Let not young souls be smothered,
 93
Let the spring sun creep, 182

Life is a feast, they say, 11
Life will finish the work, 268
Lizabetta, Marianina, Fiametta,
 Teresina, 94
Look down, O Lord, 122
Loose him and let him go, 77
Lord, give us strength, 24
Loving man, I have wearied, 216
Make of man the statue, 235
Men, my brothers, men the work-
 ers, 211
Men of England, Heirs of Glory,
 52
Men of England, wherefore plow,
 50
Men! whose boast it is that ye, 151
Mourn not the dead, 184
My church has but one temple,
 251
My country is the world, 244
My mother was a sweatshop slave,
 10
My soul was beggar, 116
Neither drugs nor charms, 47
No fledgling feeds the father bird,
 95
Not Baal, but Christus-Jingo, 111
Not in the dream of yesterday, 251
Not of the princes and prelates, 135
Now the furnaces are out, 35
Now the stone house on the lake
 front, 127
O beautiful for spacious skies, 217
O blessed voices, 272
O Brother man, 242
O Carpenter of Nazareth, 167
O China, towering, 245
O dark and cruel State, 216
O Freedom! thou art not as poets
 dream, 67
O friend! I know not which way,
 51

O God, we pray Thee for those, 189

O God, we thank Thee for this universe, 270

O Heart, that beats, 248

O Nineveh, thy realm, 71

O prairie mother, 187

O sprawling city, 127

O trade! O trade! would thou wert dead, 82

Of my city the worst that men, 98

Oh come, ye lords, 102

Oh, for a lodge in some vast wilderness, 38

On, sons of toil, 272

Once I made a political creed, 187

Or will you deem them amply paid, 143

Over his face his gray hair, 15

Over the great city, 222

Over the prairies, 230

Pent in, and sickening, 4

People singing; people with song mouths, 160

Pharaoh, Pharaoh, let my people go, 130

Redeemer of nations, 232

Riches and honor are what men desire, 46

Ring out, wild bells, 264

Sadly through the factory doors, 6

Said Christ our Lord, 145

Sail, sail thy best, 253

Salute, if you will, 184

Say not, " It matters not," 143

Say not the struggle naught availeth, 262

Shall you complain who feed the world, 85

She, being married to the soil, 26

Since the dawn of creation, 19

Slowly the gates of opportunity, 181

Snug in my easy chair, 165

So the law's agents, 117

Somewhere adown the years, 254

Sound over all waters, 203

Stoking, stoking, stoking, 16

Suddenly one day, 265

Swift gusts of hollow night, 118

Take heed of this small child, 91

Take heed that ye weep not, 137

Tell us a story to make us see, 98

Thanks to Saint Matthew, 172

The Autumn sun is shining, 169

The common street climbed up, 173

The crest and crowning of all good, 248

The Devil's auction, 169

The earth cries loud for blood, 239

The flames of God, 223

The golden age is in my heart, 233

The golf links lie so near, 96

The great machines go whirling, 170

The half-gods go, 255

The lean gray rats of hunger, 23

The law of God is one, 195

The Lord hath anointed me, 136

The martyred Christ, 48

The motor cars go up and down, 105

The Pastor says, 114

The pawn-shop man knows hunger, 21

The prison stands upon a hill, 26

The roaring of the wheels, 2

The sound of anthems, 205

The spirit of Man, 256

The thirsty of soul soon learn, 112

The touch of human hands, 176

The vestments in your church, 115

The walks are its aisles, 220

The world is led by men, 183

The worst of ills, 40

▲

Their eyelids are drooping, 39

Theirs is yon house, 59

Then I returned and saw, all oppressions, 136

There shall rise from this, 201

There's a haunting horror near us, 13

These have no Christ, 28

These things shall be, 242

They have taken the tomb, 114

They in darkness gather, 8

They looked from farmhouse windows, 78

They placed him in a prison, 239

They take up all of them, 46

They were a pattern to their age, 116

They who tread the path of labor, 237

This Beauty, this Divinity, 123

This Christmastide, America, 157

This twig — all bent, 94

Thou hast taken pledges of thy brother, 137

Though rains of jeering pelt, 227

Though starved throughout, 257

Though written vanquished, 263

Three weeks I trekked, 159

To be alive in such an age, 228

To him who is of kin to thee, 137

Tonight the beautiful, chaste moon, 10

Tremble before your chattels, 128

Two men I honor and no third, 144

'Twould please me, gods, 41

Unhappy man! uplift thine eyes, 61

Upon the skyline glows, 267

Voices, voices, they call to me, 174

We are all blind, 275

We are breaking up the molds, 197

"We are proud of death," Sacco said, 183

We are the burden-bearers, 166

We are the music makers, 247

We are they that go, 9

We builders of cities, 221

We have forgotten how to sing, 5

We have given our days, 97

"We have made them fools and weak!" 83

We have tomorrow, 119

We make iron in Birmingham, 21

We men of earth, 252

We mix from many lands, 64

We of our generation, 125

We plow and sow, 57

We praise thee, Almighty God, 260

We rest in faith, 207

We shall not travel by the road, 271

We were born of night, 87

Weep, weep, weep, 58

Well, here they are, 160

What are poets? 240

What constitutes a State, 215

What constitutes the bulwark, 269

What do you think endures, 221

What is the law of nature, 147

What is this — the sound and rumor, 62

What makes a city great, 223

What makes a nation's pillars high, 206

What strange awakening shape is this, 74

When a deed is done for Freedom, 68

When Adam delved and Eve span, 54

When I see a workingman, 81

When the psalm sings instead of the singer, 185

FIRST LINES

When the young moon faints, 17
When wilt thou save the people, 56
Where cross the crowded ways, 224
Where is the true man's father-
land, 231
Where weary folk toil, 179
Who bids for the little children, 34
Who is the patriot, 226
Whom does He love the most, 168
" Why? " — Because all I haply
can, 234
Why do the wheels go whirring
round, 11
With fingers weary and worn, 32
With instruments in ill-accord, 233

Woe unto them that decree, 45
Woe unto you who despise, 47
Would you end war, 259
Ye say to us, 'tis we who feed, 103
Ye sons of toil, 53
Ye that have faith, 260
Years of the unperformed, 208
You in whose veins runs the fire,
188
You may be Christ or Shakespeare,
178
You wear a silken undervest, 105
Your task is to form the universal,
138

ACKNOWLEDGMENTS

▲▲▲▲▲▲▲

Thanks are due to the following publishers for permission to include in this anthology the poems indicated:

Houghton Mifflin Company: Poems from the works of James Russell Lowell, Ralph Waldo Emerson, John Greenleaf Whittier, Richard Watson Gilder, William Dean Howells, William Vaughn Moody, Elizabeth Barrett Browning, Thomas Wentworth Higginson, Robert Haven Schauffler, Josephine Preston Peabody, Anna Hempstead Branch, Arlo Bates and John Drinkwater. These poems are used by permission of, and by arrangement with, Houghton Mifflin Company, the authorized publishers.

The Macmillan Company: Poems from the works of Alfred Tennyson, Robert Browning, Matthew Arnold, John Masefield, Vachel Lindsay, Wilfrid Wilson Gibson, John G. Neihardt, and Zona Gale; also the poem, "The Shadow Child," by Harriet Monroe, from the volume, "You and I"; also the selections by Stanton Coit, from the volume, "The Message of Man."

Doubleday, Doran & Company: Poems by Walt Whitman, from "Leaves of Grass," copyright, 1924, by Doubleday, Page & Company, and reprinted by special permission of Doubleday, Doran & Company, Inc., Publishers. Selections by Edward Carpenter, from "Towards Democracy."

Dodd, Mead & Company: Poems by Angela Morgan. (Copyright by Angela Morgan.)

Harper & Brothers: Two poems by Countee Cullen, by special permission. The poem, "The Voice Unto Pharaoh," by Arthur Guiterman, from "The Light Guitar," by special permission.

Henry Holt & Company: Poems by Carl Sandburg, from "Chicago Poems" and "Corn-huskers." "The Two Dwelling Places," by Romaine Rolland, from "Jean Christophe."

Coward, McCann, Inc.: The poem, "Factories," by Alfred Kreymborg, from "Manhattan Men." Copyright, 1929, Coward, McCann, Inc.

Edwin Markham: Ten copyright poems from "The Collected Poems of Edwin Markham," in preparation. Used by special permission of Edwin Markham.

Charles Scribner's Sons: Poems by Henry van Dyke, from his poetical works, copyright by Charles Scribner's Sons. The poem, "The Call of

ACKNOWLEDGMENTS

▲

Brotherhood," by Corinne Roosevelt Robinson, copyright, 1911, by Charles Scribner's Sons. The lines entitled "Trade," by Sidney Lanier, from "The Symphony," copyright by Charles Scribner's Sons.

Cornhill Publishing Company: The poem, "The Hungry," by Caroline Giltinan.

Brandt & Brandt: Two poems, "Roses in the Subway" and "Paper Roses," from "Poems by Dana Burnet," copyright, 1915, by Harper & Brothers.

The Argus Book Shop: Five poems by John Davidson.

Funk & Wagnalls Company: The extract, "The Collection," from "Swords and Plowshares," by Ernest Crosby, by special permission of the publishers, Funk & Wagnalls Company, New York.

Harcourt, Brace & Company: Selections from "Smoke and Steel" and "Work Gangs," from the volume, "Smoke and Steel"; used by special permission. Two poems by Margaret Widdemer, from "The Factories and Other Poems," copyright Harcourt, Brace & Company. The poem, "Caliban in the Coal Mines," by Louis Untermeyer, from the volume, "Challenge," published and copyrighted by Harcourt, Brace & Company.

Horace Liveright: The poem, "He Whom a Dream Hath Possessed," from the volume, "Jealous of Dead Leaves," by Shaemas O'Sheel, copyright by Horace Liveright, Publisher. The Poem, "Fulfilling," from the volume, "Machinery," by MacKnight Black, published by Horace Liveright. The poem, "Piccadilly," by Ezra Pound, from his published works, copyright by Horace Liveright.

Alfred A. Knopf, Inc.: The poems, "We Have Tomorrow," "I, Too," and "The Negro," reprinted from the volumes, "Weary Blues" and "Fine Clothes to the Jew," by Langston Hughes, by special permission of the publishers, Alfred A. Knopf, Inc.

The Viking Press: The two selections, "The Golden Age" and "I Served in a Great Cause," from "Poems of Justice," by Horace Traubel: New York: The Viking Press, Inc.: Copyright, 1912, by B. W. Huebsch, Inc. The poem, "To the Free Children," from "Red Flag," by Lola Ridge: Copyright, 1927, by the Viking Press, New York.

Longmans, Green & Company: Three poems by William Morris, from his published works. Permission has been secured from the trustees of the estate of William Morris.

Henry Harrison, Publisher: The poems, "The Rulers," by Davies; "Invocation," by Plotkin; "Pride," by Henry Harrison; "Failures," by Trent, reprinted from "The Sacco-Vanzetti Anthology of Verse," published by Henry Harrison. Used by special permission of the publisher.

[304]

ACKNOWLEDGMENTS

National Child Labor Committee, New York: The poems, "The Prop" and "The Price of Sugar," by Frances Williams; "The Working Child to the Story Teller," by Laura Benet, "The Immigrant Madonna," by Helen Dwight Fisher; "The Little Children," by Irwin Granich: Reprinted from "Poems of Child Labor," by special permission.

A. M. Robertson, Publisher: Two poems by George Sterling, "In the Market-Place" and "The New State," used by special permission of A. M. Robertson, who holds the copyright on the works of George Sterling.

The Pilgrim Press: The selections by Walter Rauschenbusch from the volume, "Prayers of the Social Awakening," by Walter Rauschenbusch. Copyright by The Pilgrim Press. Used by permission.

Lothrop, Lee & Shepard: The poem, "The Sweat Shop," by Richard Burton, from the volume, "Message and Melody," published by Lothrop, Lee & Shepard, Boston.

Thomas Y. Crowell Company: The extract from "Reading Gaol," by Oscar Wilde.

D. Appleton & Company: The extract from "Manhattan," by Charles Hanson Towne, from "Selected Poems."

Acknowledgment is made also to the following magazines for permission to reprint the poems indicated:

The New Masses: "Mine-Song," by E. Falkowski.

The Outlook: "Hammer and Nails," by Kenneth W. Porter. "The New City," by Marguerite Wilkinson.

The Nation: "We Make Iron in Birmingham," by Karl Harrison.

Life: "The March of the Hungry Men."

Christian Science Sentinel: "Vision," by Anne C. Cheney.

The American Federationist: "On, Sons of Toil," by Thornton Oakley.

Unity: "To a Student," by E. K. Biddle; "Prayer for Spring," by Sylvia Hill.

The World Tomorrow: "Woman Plowing," by Robert Liddell Lowe.

Poetry: A Magazine of Verse; "The Lean Gray Rats," by Skipwith Cannell.

The Survey: "Blind," by June Lucas; "Martyrdom," by Leonard van Noppen.

The Christian Century: Poems by Raymond Kresensky, Lee Spencer, Thomas Curtis Clark, Verne Bright, Brent Dow Allison, Edgar Frank, Cyprus R. Mitchell, Edward Shillito, Richard M. Steiner, Tertius van Dyke, Marion M. Wildman, Kathryn Wright, Gertrude B. Gunderson, Charles Granville Hamilton, Aubert Edgar Bruce, Howard McKinley Corning, Earl Marlatt, Maurice Rowntree, Edwin M. Poteat, Jr., Jay G. Sigmund, William L. Stidger and Herman W. Stillman.

ACKNOWLEDGMENTS

The Commonweal: "Profit or Loss," by William M. Gilbert.
Contemporary Verse: Poems by Lucia Trent and Ralph Cheyney.

Thanks are due also to the following poets, for personal cooperation in allowing the use of their poems: Florence Wilkinson Evans, Countee Cullen, Carl Sandburg, Upton Sinclair, Mary Craig Sinclair, Zona Gale, Hermann Hagedorn, Elias Lieberman, Vachel Lindsay, John G. Neihardt, James Weldon Johnson, Langston Hughes, Edwin Markham, Raymond Kresensky, James Oppenheim, Cyprus R. Mitchell, Lola Ridge, Florence Kiper Frank, Elizabeth Waddell, June Lucas, Robert Whitaker, Anna Louise Strong (through Sidney Strong), Katharine Lee Bates (through her estate), Kenneth W. Porter, Vida D. Scudder, Hugh Francis Blunt, Harry Kemp, Lucia Trent, Ralph Cheyney, Clement Wood, Charlotte Perkins Gilman, Berton Braley, Ralph Chaplin, Sarah Cleghorn, Helen Gray Cone, Richard Warner Borst, Leonard Van Noppen, Henry van Dyke, Dana Burnet, Anne Cleveland Cheney, Hortense Flexner, Charles Erskine Scott Wood, Sara Bard Field, Margaret Widdemer, Harriet Monroe, John Curtis Underwood, Robert Haven Schauffler, Louise Driscoll, Frank Mason North, Lee Spencer, William Dudley Foulke, Miles M. Dawson, Mary Carolyn Davies, Arthur Guiterman, Karl C. Harrison, Richard Burton, Felix Adler, Albert Bigelow Paine, Charles Hanson Towne, Louis Ginsberg, Henry Harrison, Ernest Hartsock, Mary Sinton Leitch, Ruth LePrade, Robert Liddell Lowe, Shaemas O'Sheel, Angela Morgan, Lewis Worthington Smith, Fanny Bixby Spencer, George S. Viereck, D. Maitland Bushby, Mary Carolyn Davies, and Willard Wattles.